New Testament

JESUS CHRIST:
HIS LIFE AND HIS CHURCH

to Maurice
with every blessing
+ John Rack

The SPCK International Study Guides incorporate the much loved and respected TEF series, and follow the tradition of clarity and simplicity; a worldwide, ecumenical perspective; and an emphasis on application of the material studied, drawing out its relevance for Christians today. The Guides are ideal for students and Bible study groups, as well as for multi-cultural classes, and students for whom English is a second language.

ISG Study Guide 24

New Testament Introduction 1
JESUS CHRIST:
HIS LIFE AND HIS CHURCH

Margaret Baxter

First published in Great Britain in 1987

Society for Promoting Christian Knowledge
36 Causton Street
London SW1P 4ST

© Margaret Baxter 1987

The photographs are reproduced by courtesy of the British Library (p. 4)
the British/Israel Public Affairs Committee (pp. 8a & b, 18h, and 33a),
the Mansell Collection (p. 25),
USPG (pp. 33b, 43a, 54, 62, 71a, 77a, and 104a),
the Bible Society (p. 89a & b),
Lee/Dennis, Methodist Information (p. 104b),
Barnaby's Picture Library (p. 110b),
Campaign for Nuclear Disarmament (p. 115),
Christian Aid (p. 121b), and Camera Press Ltd. ·

British Library Cataloguing-in-Publication Data
A catalogue record for this book is available from
the British Library

ISBN 978-0-281-04315-6

9 10

First printed and bound in Great Britain by
Latimer Trend & Company Ltd, Plymouth
Reprinted in Great Britain by
Ashford Colour Press

Produced on paper from sustainable forests

Contents

Preface

I should like to express grateful acknowledgements for the help and advice that I have received from so many people. In particular I want to thank:

The students of the Sierra Leone Church Training Centre and Theological Hall who taught me so much, and without whom this book would not have been conceived, and the colleagues who encouraged my efforts.

The staff of SPCK, without whom it would have remained no more than an idea in the mind. My thanks go especially to Nick Beddow for his enthusiasm and encouragement, and to Daphne Terry for her attention to detail.

Stuart, Ruth, Mary and Paul for their patience over several years.

Those who over the years have shared their own enthusiasm for the study of theology, and encouraged me to do the same. My thanks to David Hinson, whose Introduction to the Old Testament in this series has been a useful teaching aid and provided me with a number of ideas.

The following people who kindly gave their time and their expertise to read the manuscript, and sent their comments and suggestions: The Reverend Dr C. K. Barrett, Professor Emeritus of Durham University; The Rt Reverend Dr R. P. C. Hanson, Professor Emeritus of Manchester University; The Reverend Canon John Hargreaves; The Reverend Canon Rodney Hunter of Zomba Theological College, Malawi; The Reverend Dr Mathew John, Principal of Bishop's College, Calcutta. Their comments were of great value and all have been given careful consideration.

My hope is that this book will be useful for those who are studying the New Testament for the first time, and that it will encourage them to go on to further study at much greater depth.

Nelson, Lancashire   MARGARET BAXTER

About This Book

This is the first volume in a two-volume introduction to the New Testament. The first volume contains an account of events beginning with Jesus Christ and ending with the leaders of the early Church writing letters to Christians. The second volume begins with the writing of the Gospels, and traces the events which have led to our reading the New Testament in modern translations.

AN INTRODUCTION

In the study of theology 'introduction' is often used as a technical expression which refers to questions such as 'Who wrote this book?', 'When did he write it?', 'For whom did he write it?'. Some of these questions are touched upon in these volumes, but they are chiefly meant to provide an 'introduction' in the more usual and general sense. They introduce readers to the background as well as the contents of the New Testament, discuss different aspects of its teaching and interpretation, and show how it reached its present form. Many books contain technical words without fully explaining them. (This is not only a problem of theology; every subject has its own specialized language.) In this Guide we explain most of the technical terms as we go along.

SPECIAL NOTES

The two Special Notes in this volume, about dates and cross-references, are separate from the rest of the text because they relate to more than one section of the book. Readers may want to read them first, to read them as they work through the book, or to leave them out altogether.

STUDY SUGGESTIONS

Most chapters in the book are divided into two or three sections, with study suggestions at the end of each section.
There are four kinds of study suggestion:
Words and Meanings: These are to help readers check their understanding of the words used.
Review of Content: These questions are to help readers check their progress, and discover whether they have remembered and understood what they have read.
Bible Study: These are to help readers to discover for themselves why the coming of Jesus was said to 'fulfil the scripture', and relate the teaching of the apostles with that in other parts of the Bible and with the words of Jesus Himself. Questions requiring use of a concordance

or Bible dictionary are intended for students who possess such books or have access to a library.

Further Study and Discussion: These are to help readers to do further study and to think out the practical application of what has been learned. They are especially useful for group discussions.

The *Key* (p. 131) will enable readers to check their own work on those questions which can be checked in that way.

TECHNICAL TERMS

Appendix 1 (p. 128) provides concise definitions of the technical terms which have been used.

USEFUL ABBREVIATIONS

Appendix 2 (p. 129) 'translates' the various abbreviations used. It also includes some common abbreviations which are not used in this book, but which readers are likely to meet in reference books and other books of theology.

MAPS

The maps of Palestine and of the Eastern Mediterranean in New Testament times (pp. x and 83) provide a general picture of the geographical background to chapters 1–4 and 5–8 respectively.

INDEX

The index includes most of the subjects dealt with in this book, and the names of important people and places mentioned.

BIBLE VERSION

This Guide is based upon the Revised Standard Version of the Bible Ecumenical Edition.

HELPS TO BIBLE STUDY

Students will also find the following books helpful:

1. *A Concordance*, which is an alphabetical list of words and names used in the Bible, with references to show the books, chapters and verses where they may be found. A concordance is usually related to a version of the Bible, e.g. *The Concise Concordance to the NRSV* (OUP). Students of the Bible find it very helpful to have a concordance of their own.

2. *A Bible Dictionary* contains articles on the topics, places and people which are found in the Bible, e.g. 'sabbaths'. Most theological libraries have at least one Bible dictionary.

3. *Commentaries*. Most commentaries deal with a single book of the Bible (e.g. the Gospel of Mark), which is explained chapter by chapter.

There are also some one-volume commentaries which deal with every book in the Bible, and contain general articles about the Bible. For general study of the Bible a one-volume commentary is a very useful book to possess.

4. *Other ISG Guides.* Some of the subjects which are introduced in this Guide, as well as some individual books of the Bible, are treated in greater depth in other ISG Guides.

FURTHER READING

INTRODUCTORY BOOKS

E. Charpentier, *How to Read the New Testament* (SCM Press, 1982).

Bruce Chilton, *Beginning New Testament Study* (SPCK, 1986).

John Drane, *Introducing the New Testament* (revised edition, Lion, 1999).

Kenneth Grayston, *The New Testament: Which Way In?* (Darton, Longman & Todd, 2000).

H. Wayne House, *Chronological and Background Charts of the New Testament* (Zondervan, 1981).

Justin Taylor, *Where Did Christianity Come From?* (Liturgical Press, 2001).

MORE ADVANCED

Schuyler Brown, *The Origins of Christianity: A Historical Introduction to the New Testament* (revised edition, OUP, 1993).

Craig A. Evans and Stanley E. Porter (eds), *Dictionary of New Testament Background* (IVP,2000)

K. C. Hanson and Douglas E. Oakman, *Palestine in the Time of Jesus* (Fortress Press, 1998).

Steve Moyise, *The Old Testament in the New Testament: An Introduction* (Continuum, 2001).

Christopher Tuckett, *Reading the New Testament: Methods of Interpretation* (SPCK,1987).

USEFUL REFERENCE BOOKS

Concise Oxford Dictionary of the Christian Church (OUP)
The New Bible Dictionary (IVP)
Oxford Bible Atlas (OUP)
The Concise Concordance to the NRSV (OUP)

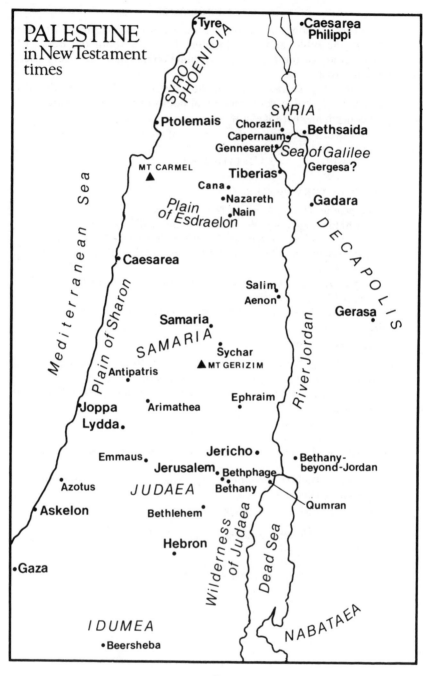

PALESTINE
in New Testament
times

Tyre
Caesarea Philippi

SYRO-PHOENICIA

SYRIA

Ptolemais
Chorazin
Capernaum
Gennesaret
Bethsaida
Sea of Galilee
Gergesa?

MT CARMEL ▲
Cana
Tiberias
Nazareth
Nain
Gadara

Plain of Esdraelon

DECAPOLIS

Mediterranean Sea

Caesarea

Salim
Aenon

Gerasa

Samaria

SAMARIA

Sychar
▲ MT GERIZIM

Plain of Sharon

Antipatris

River Jordan

Ephraim

Joppa
Lydda

Arimathea

Jericho
Emmaus
Jerusalem
Bethphage
Bethany-beyond-Jordan

Azotus
JUDAEA
Bethany

Askelon
Bethlehem

Qumran

Wilderness of Judaea

Dead Sea

Hebron

Gaza

IDUMEA

NABATAEA

Beersheba

1

Introduction:
The Bible as the Word of God

'For the word of God is living and active, sharper than any two-edged sword, piercing to the division of soul and spirit, of joints and marrow, and discerning the thoughts and intentions of the heart' (Heb. 4.12).

In our different Churches and Christian groups we use various words and phrases to mean the Bible. We call it the 'Holy Bible' and 'Scripture'. Both these names originally had ordinary meanings. 'Scripture' meant 'something written', although it has come to mean a sacred book ('script' still means handwriting). 'Bible' comes from a Greek word meaning 'books'. At its simplest level 'Holy Bible' means 'books which belong to God'.

In many Churches readings from the Bible are ended with the reader saying, 'This is the word of the Lord.' In all Churches it is common to call the Bible, 'the Word of God'. What do we mean when we use this phrase?

THAT LITTLE WORD 'OF'

If we use the Shorter Oxford Dictionary and look up 'of' we shall find that it gives seventeen different meanings. Here we consider three meanings which it could have when the Bible is called 'the Word of God':

1. '*About*', as used in the sentence, 'Have you had any news *of* Moses Kamara?'

The Bible is certainly a book *about* God. It tells what God has done and what His purposes are. For us as Christians the Bible is the main source for learning about God. In the New Testament alone the word 'God' is used over 1,200 times. Jesus talked about God His Father and the Kingdom of God.

2. '*Spoken by*', as used in the sentence, 'You can trust the word *of* an honest man.'

Some of the words in the Bible were obviously spoken *by* God (e.g. 'A voice from heaven saying, "This is my beloved Son, with whom I am well pleased."' Matt. 3.17). However, it is often clear that the words we read were spoken by someone else, Peter, or Pilate, or a blind person wanting Jesus to heal him.

Some Christians think that God 'spoke' *all* the words in the Bible, and that men like Mark, John and Paul simply wrote them down. This

1

is a very comforting way of looking at the Bible. The problem comes when the Bible seems to disagree with itself. According to Mark, Jesus said, 'Whoever divorces his wife and marries another, commits adultery against her' (Mark 10.11). According to Matthew He said, 'Every one who divorces his wife, except on the ground of unchastity, makes her an adulteress' (Matt. 5.32). How are we to account for this difference? In one of his letters Paul stated plainly that he was giving his own opinion: 'Now concerning the unmarried, I have no command of the Lord, but I give my opinion as one who by the Lord's mercy is trustworthy' (1 Cor. 7.25, see p. 96).

'Of' does not often mean 'spoken by', and there are good reasons for thinking that 'the Word of God' means more than 'words spoken by God'.

3. *'Belonging to'*, as used in the phrase 'the law *of* the land'.

'Of' is commonly used to mean possession – 'the roof of the house', 'the uniform of the school'. To say that the Bible is the Word of God could mean that it *belongs to* God. It is God's possession, under His control. God has a special and close relationship with the Bible. It is His book, and He uses it.

WHAT IS A WORD?

One person speaks a word, and another person hears it. If we hear someone shout, 'Look out!' we shall probably turn around. Those two small words have brought a message that there is danger of some sort. A teacher lines children up for a race and shouts, 'Ready! Steady! Go!' Each of these words is a signal which the children understand. When they hear 'Go!' they start to run.

A word is a way of communicating. There are other ways of communicating which do not use words. Members of certain societies use special greetings to communicate the fact that they belong to that society. Ships use flags to carry messages: one plain yellow flag means that everyone on board is healthy, two yellow flags means that someone has an infectious disease, and a blue flag with a white square in the middle means that everyone should get on board, for the ship is about to leave the harbour. Messages can be sent by flashing lights. Three short flashes followed by three long flashes and then three more short flahes is the international signal which means, 'I am in trouble. Help me!' North American Indians sent messages in puffs of smoke. Many African peoples use talking drums.

So we see that it is possible to communicate without using words at all. Even if two people meet and neither of them understands the language of the other, they find ways of communicating without using words. But they only have a limited means of communication. They will find they can communicate much better with each other if there is

2

another language which they can both speak. Most communication between human beings is by using words. We talk to our families and friends. We listen to preachers, teachers, politicians. We listen to the radio, and read books and newspapers. All these things depend on words. Words exist so that we can communicate.

If a word is a way of communicating, then the Word of God means God's way of communicating. We call the Bible the Word of God, because it is a message from God which tells us what He is like, and how He wants people to live.

JESUS AS THE WORD OF GOD

'In the beginning was the Word, and the Word was with God, and the Word was God. He was in the beginning with God' (John 1.1.–2). As Christians, we believe that God has shown us what He is like. To put it in more theological language, God has 'revealed' Himself. He reveals Himself in the Bible, but He has revealed Himself in an even more important way.

The opening verses of John's Gospel are about the Word of God. Clearly when John wrote about 'the Word' he meant Jesus, who is God's way of communicating with us. 'The only Son, who is in the bosom of the Father, he has made him known' (John 1.18). God has revealed Himself in Jesus. The writer to the Hebrews put the same idea in another way. 'In many and various ways God spoke to our fathers by the prophets; but in these last days he has spoken to us by a Son, whom he appointed the heir of all things, through whom also he created the world' (Heb. 1.1–2).

In Jesus God shows us His great love: 'In this the love of God was made manifest among us, that God sent his only Son into the world' (1 John 4.9). Through the example and teaching of Jesus God has made clear the way He wants people to live. Through the power of the risen Jesus He guides and strengthens His children every day. 'You have been born anew ... through the living and abiding word of God' (1 Peter 1.23). It is Jesus Himself who is the living and abiding Word of God.

THE BIBLE AS THE WORD OF GOD

Above all God has spoken to us in Jesus. The Bible is His word in a secondary sense. In order to meet Jesus we turn to the Bible. There we can read about Jesus, about His life, His death and His resurrection. We can read how the lives of His followers were completely changed by what happened, and how they lived afterwards. The Bible is essential to us as Christians, and we are right to call it the Word of God. Jesus Himself is God's message to mankind, but the Bible brings that message to us.

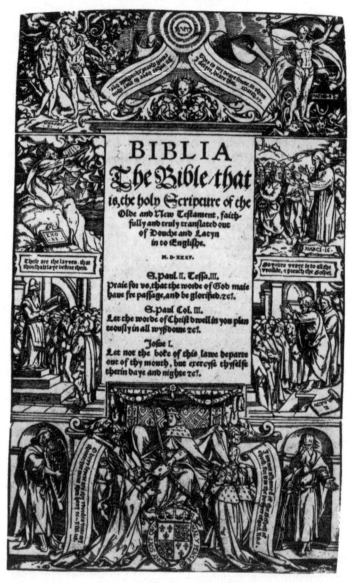

'The Bible is essential to us as Christians', and today most Christians can read it in their own tongue: The New Testament or parts of it have been put into some 1,950 different languages. But in English there was no full translation until the year 1382. The title-page above is dated 1535, when Coverdale's printed version first made the complete Bible widely available to English readers.

JEWISH AND MUSLIM IDEAS ABOUT THE WORD OF GOD

For Christians the Word of God is primarily a person. For Jews and Muslims it is a book.

1. *The Jewish Word.* For Jews the Word of God is above all the 'Torah', the Law of Moses. We find the Torah in the first five books of the Old Testament. Jews believe that God 'spoke' the Law, and Moses was the messenger who wrote the words down and carried them to the people. Every Jewish boy must learn to recite at least a part of the Law in Hebrew, because when God spoke He spoke in Hebrew.

Jews think of Moses as a great man, a prophet, a saint, the founder of the nation, but they do not think of Moses himself as the revelation of God. Moses was the one who brought the message. It is the book, the Torah, which is seen as the Word of God and held in the highest honour.

2. *The Muslim Word.* For Muslims the Word of God is the *Qur'an.* The Qur'an contains the very words of Allah (the Arabic name for God) himself, which have existed from eternity. Allah, they believe, spoke the words in Arabic, the Angel Gabriel told them to the prophet Muhammad who recited them, and his followers wrote them down. Every Muslim must learn to recite the words of the Qur'an. When a Muslim prays, he recites chapters of 'God's Words'. The Qur'an must always be in Arabic, because according to Muslim belief Arabic is the language of God.

Muhammad is acknowledged as a great man, the founder of Islam, the Seal of the prophets. Muslims honour and revere him, and follow his example. Yet to a Muslim Muhammad is always of less importance than the Qur'an itself. Like Moses, Muhammad was only the messenger, not the message.

THREE BOOKS AND THREE MEN

Judaism, Christianity and Islam are three great and closely related religions. All three have a founder. All three have holy books. Yet Christians do not hold their holy book in the same sort of honour as Jews and Muslims do theirs. Also Christians worship Jesus, while Jews and Muslims would consider it a great sin to worship Moses or Muhammad.

These facts often lead to misunderstanding, especially between Muslims and Christians. According to the Qur'an Jesus is a prophet who brought the gospel. Muslims expect Christians to treat the Bible in the same way as Muslims treat the Qur'an. A Muslim is horrified when he sees a Christian writing in his Bible, or putting it on the floor, or laying another book on top of it. He finds it very strange that so many translations of the Bible exist, and that Christians read it in their own language, instead of in the language in which it was written. Some

Christians too are troubled by these things, especially if they live in a country where there are many Muslims.

It all comes back to what we believe about the Word of God and the way we think God has revealed Himself and His will. As Christians we do not believe that Jesus came to bring us the Bible, or the New Testament, or even the gospel. We believe that He Himself is God, and that He came to reveal God to us.

For a Jew, God has spoken in the Law.

For a Muslim, God has spoken in the Qur'an.

For a Christian, God has spoken in Jesus.

The difference can be summed up in this way:

Religion	Word by which God has spoken	Messenger or bearer of the Word
Judaism	The Law	Moses
Islam	The Qur'an	Muhammad
Christianity	Jesus	The Bible

SCRIPTURES

All the major 'developed' religions have their sacred books. Mathew John, an Indian theologian, reminds us that Hindus have the Vedas and Upanishads and other books. The most popular book among Hindus is perhaps the *Bhagavad Gita*, although it does not belong to the Vedas. Hindus believe that the Vedas are eternal, not the result of human activity. For Theravada Buddhists the authoritative scriptures are the *Tripitaka*, or 'The Three Baskets'. These contain the traditions about the life and teaching of their founder. The Sikhs have the *Granth Saheb*, which contains the teachings of the early gurus, and Parsees have the *Zend Avesta*.

CHRISTIANS AND THE BIBLE

The importance of the Bible to Christians is that in the New Testament we come face to face with Jesus. In the twentieth century it is our main source for knowing Jesus and understanding Him. It brings us God's message, and we hold it in high honour. It is not only about God. It belongs to God, and He uses it to speak to people today. The study of the Bible, especially the New Testament, is meant to bring us to Christ, so that we can hear His call and follow Him, as the first disciples did. We are free to write in our Bibles if it helps us. We are free to translate the Bible into all the languages of the world. Our distinctive Christian belief is that God did not speak to us in Hebrew or Arabic or any other ancient language. He spoke to us in Jesus.

Because it is Jesus who is above all the Word of God, we shall begin our study of the New Testament by looking at Jesus Himself.

STUDY SUGGESTIONS

WORDS AND MEANINGS

1. What did these words originally mean: (a) 'Scripture', (b) 'Bible'?
2. What do we mean when we say that God has 'revealed' Himself?

REVIEW OF CONTENT

3. What three different meanings could the word 'of' have, in the phrase 'The Word of God'?
4. What is the purpose of words?
5. What is the 'Word of God':
   (a) for a Jew?   (b) for a Muslim?   (c) for a Christian?

BIBLE STUDY

6. Read John 1.1–18. In which verses does the writer state that:
   (a) The Word has always existed?
   (b) God used the Word to create the world?
   (c) The Word is the source of life?
   (d) The Word is a light which has come into the world?
   (e) The Word became a human being?
   (f) Some people rejected Him?
   (g) Other people saw the glory of God in Him?
   (h) The Word is the Son who has made God known to us?
7. What is meant by 'the Word', in each of the following verses?
   (a) Acts 6.2   (b) 2 Cor. 4.2   (c) Titus 2.5
   (d) 2 Peter 3.5   (e) 1 John 2.14   (f) Rev. 19.13
8. How can you explain the difference between the two accounts of the teaching of Jesus given in Matthew 5.32 and Mark 10.11?

FURTHER STUDY AND DISCUSSION

9. Communicating without words is called 'non-verbal communication'. Describe some examples of non-verbal communication.
10. Having read this chapter, what do you now think is the meaning of the verse quoted at the beginning (Hebrews 4.12)? Is it the same as you thought when you started the chapter?
11. When the members of your Church call the Bible 'the Word of God', what do you think they mean? Do they all mean the same thing? Do you agree with their ideas? Give your reasons.
12. Write a letter to explain to a Muslim why Christians feel free to write in their Bibles, but would not call a child 'Jesus Christ'.

Though Jesus was born in Bethlehem, His home was in Nazareth, seen above as it is today. Both places are visited by thousands of pilgrims every year – as witness the 'Welcome to Bethlehem' notice below. But Nazareth is still only a small town, and Bethlehem little more than a large village.

2
Jesus: His Land and His People

LIFE AT HOME

'Jesus went down with them and came to Nazareth, and was obedient to them; and his mother kept all these things in her heart' (Luke 2.51).

Jesus lived in Galilee, a small country on the edge of the Roman Empire. His home town was Nazareth, a small town of no importance. His parents were ordinary working people. His father was a carpenter, who probably worked long hours to provide for the needs of his family. His mother too worked hard, carrying the water, going to market, grinding corn, cooking, cleaning, spinning, weaving and sewing, just as millions of women have always done and still do in many countries of the world today.

THE HOUSE

Jesus and His family probably lived in a small one-roomed house with a flat roof, made of mud bricks. Not many houses in Palestine had an upstairs room. When they did, it was something to be noticed. Jesus ate His last meal with His disciples in a 'large upper room'. Probably it was a room built on the flat roof of a house and reached by an outside staircase. The flat roofs were useful places for drying crops and for saying prayers.

Inside the house it would have been dark and cool. The houses did not have many windows. The single room was divided into two areas, one part being a raised platform. The lower part was where the animals were kept at night. At other times the children could play and adults could work there. The family used the raised part for eating and sleeping. They slept on mats which they rolled up and put away during the day-time. There was very little furniture, but there were spaces built into the thickness of the walls. These recesses were used as shelves and places for storing things. There was a place for the cooking pots to be stored, and another place for the sleeping mats. Perhaps a high recess was for the lamp, which was a small dish filled with olive oil with a linen wick. A wooden chest probably held the family's most treasured possessions.

FOOD

The Jewish people ate simple meals. Their basic food was bread, made from wheat or barley flour. The women used little stone mills to grind the grain and make it into flour. Oil, for cooking and for use in the lamps, was pressed from olives. Water was the usual drink, with wine on special occasions.

'Basic to all the needs of man's life are water and fire and iron and salt and wheat flour and milk and honey, the blood of the grape, and oil and clothing' (Sirach 39.26). These words were probably written by a Jew in the middle of the first century BC, and were included in the writings of the Apocrypha (see Vol. 2). Meat was a luxury, eaten on feast days, but people who lived near the sea or the Lake of Galilee could eat fish. The lad who gave his food to Jesus had five barley loaves and two fish (John 6.9). People who could afford to do so ate twice a day, at midday and in the evening.

CLOTHING

Clothes were made of linen, cotton or wool. If the cloth was dyed it was more expensive. The New Testament writers used various words to describe the garments which people wore:

1. A *coat* or *tunic*, e.g. Jesus's seamless tunic (John 19.23). This was an under-garment. Sometimes it was woven in a single piece on a wide loom. It could also be made on a narrow loom in three pieces which had to be sewn together.

2. An *outer garment*, e.g. Jesus's garments which became shining white at the transfiguration (Matt. 17.2). For most people this was just an oblong piece of cloth, worn as a cloak in the day-time, and wrapped around themselves as a blanket at night.

3. A *mantle* or *robe*, e.g. the best robe which the father put on the prodigal son (Luke 15.22). Such a garment probably had sleeves, and was a mark of distinction, worn by people of importance.

4. A *girdle*, e.g. the leather girdle worn by John the Baptist (Mark 1.6). A girdle was a long folded sash, which was used as a money belt and to hold in the flowing robes.

Women's clothes were probably very similar, although they also wore a veil to cover their hair (1 Cor. 11.5).

A GOD-FEARING FAMILY

Jesus's parents were Jews. Joseph could trace his ancestors back to the great king David, and Mary's cousin Elizabeth was married to a priest (Luke 1.5, 36; 2.4). According to Luke, Jesus was brought up in the usual Jewish customs. He was circumcised on the eighth day. When He was almost six weeks old Joseph and Mary went to Jerusalem so that they could present their baby son to God in the Temple, and make the sacrifice that the Jewish law commanded. Joseph and Mary went to Jerusalem every year to celebrate the feast of Passover. From the time Jesus was twelve years old He went with them (Luke 2.21–41).

So Jesus grew up in a home where God was worshipped, and His law

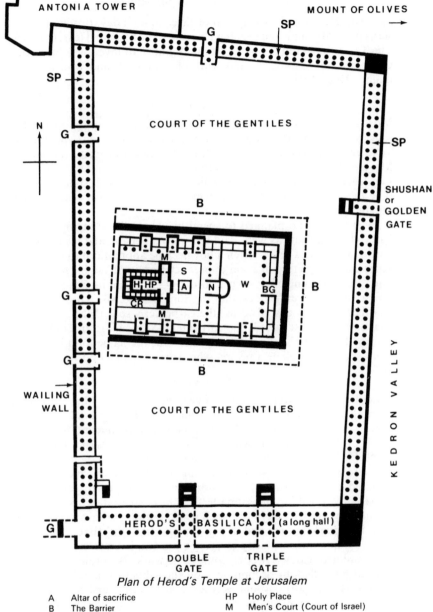

Plan of Herod's Temple at Jerusalem

A	Altar of sacrifice	HP	Holy Place
B	The Barrier	M	Men's Court (Court of Israel)
BG	Beautiful Gate	N	Nicanor Gate
CR	Council Room, for Sanhedrin	S	Sanctuary (Court for priests only)
G	Gates	SP	Solomon's Portico
H	Holy of Holies	W	Women's Court

11

was kept. He learned to pray two or three times a day, turning to face Jerusalem. Morning and evening He recited the Shema: 'Hear, O Israel: The LORD our God is one LORD; and you shall love the LORD your God with all your heart, and with all your soul, and with all your might' (Deut. 6.4).

SCHOOL AND WORK

Most Jewish boys went to school. The synagogues ran schools in the same sort of way that mosques and some Churches do, and for the same reasons. The boys had to learn to read and recite the law of Moses. They sat on the floor around their teacher. Until the age of ten they learned only the Scriptures which we call the Old Testament. After that they could begin to learn what the great Jewish teachers had taught.

Even a boy who planned to spend his whole life studying the Law had to learn a trade as well. Paul was such a person, and his trade was tent-making (Acts 18.3). Often a boy became apprenticed to his father. Jesus used the picture of a son-apprentice learning from his father: 'the Son can do nothing of his own accord, but only what he sees the Father doing; for whatever he does, that the Son does likewise' (John 5.19). In Matthew Jesus is described as 'the carpenter's son' (Matt. 13.55). In Mark Jesus is just called 'the carpenter' (Mark 6.3). Probably Jesus learned His father's trade. A 'carpenter' was the name for a builder or stone-mason as well as a person who worked with wood.

SABBATHS

School and work were enough to keep any boy busy, but on Friday evening all work stopped. From sunset on Friday until sunset on Saturday was the sabbath. The Law commanded that no one should work on the sabbath. It was a day of rest, remembering God's rest when He had completed the work of creation.

There was a lot of discussion among the Jews about which activities counted as work. A number of stories in the Gospels are about Jesus apparently 'breaking the sabbath'. It is possible that 'work' had once meant farming. 'Six days you shall work, but on the seventh you shall rest; in ploughing time and in harvest you shall rest' (Exod. 34.21). In Jesus's time 'work' included carrying a burden. Even to carry a pen, or for a tailor to carry a needle, counted as work. Naturally a man who carried his rolled-up sleeping mat on the sabbath was told, 'It is not lawful' (John 5.10). No-one was allowed to walk further than three-quarters of a mile on the sabbath, which led to the expression 'a sabbath day's journey' (see Acts 1.12). When Jesus's disciples picked and ate some ears of grain on a sabbath day, the Pharisees asked why they were doing something that was not lawful (Luke 6.1–12). To pick the ears counted as reaping, to rub the husks off counted as threshing.

The sabbath was more than a day for not working. It was also a day for relaxing with family and friends. On Friday night a family enjoyed eating their sabbath meal together. It was on a Saturday (sabbath) that Jesus visited Peter's home and healed his mother-in-law (Mark 1.21–31). Another sabbath He dined at the home of a Pharisee (Luke 14.1–6). More than anything else, the sabbath was the day when a Jew went to the synagogue (see p. 16).

LANGUAGES

'He said to her, "Talitha cumi"; which means, "Little girl, I say to you, arise"' (Mark 5.41). '*Talitha cumi*' is Aramaic. Aramaic was the everyday language used by Jews living in Palestine in the first century AD, but it was only one of four languages that were used:

1. *Hebrew*: Hebrew is the language in which most of the Old Testament is written. It was the language of Israel until the time when the Jews went into exile. It was the language of scripture, so eventually it came to be thought of as a sacred language. Every Jewish boy learned to read Hebrew, but we have no way of knowing how many people could speak it in Jesus' day. When the Old Testament scripture was read in Hebrew, it used to be translated into Aramaic so that people could understand it.

2. *Aramaic*: There was a group of Aramaic languages, closely related to Hebrew, and even more closely related to each other. About 300 years before Jesus lived the Jewish people were ruled by the Persians. Aramaic was the official language of the Persian Empire, and it came to be spoken in all the countries they had ruled. In the 5th century BC Nehemiah complained that many Jewish children 'could not speak the language of Judah', i.e. Hebrew (Neh. 13.24). Jesus spoke Aramaic, and a few of His Aramaic words have been kept in the New Testament (see Mark 5.41). It is likely that in many places in the New Testament where we read 'the Hebrew language' or 'in Hebrew' it actually means Aramaic, the everyday language that the Hebrews had come to speak.

3. *Greek*: Greek was introduced into Palestine about 300 years before Jesus was born. The Greek king Alexander the Great conquered Persia and Egypt, and led his armies as far as India. He and the Greek rulers who followed him did everything they could to spread the language and culture of Greece. Greek became the common language of the countries around the eastern Mediterranean Sea. Greek cities were built in many places. In Egypt Alexandria became a centre of Greek culture and learning. There were Greek cities in Galilee, and Jesus could probably speak Greek. The woman from Syrophoenicia would have spoken to Him in Greek, and so would the Greeks who went looking for Him in Jerusalem (Mark 7.24–30; John 12.20–21).

The everyday Greek which ordinary people spoke was called the 'koine', common Greek, as distinct from classical and literary Greek. The New Testament was written in koine Greek.

4. *Latin*: Latin was the language spoken by the Romans, and the official language of the Roman Empire. Official notices were written in Latin. Ordinary people in the eastern part of the Roman Empire knew only a little Latin, so notices were probably written in Greek as well. According to John the Roman governor of Judaea put a notice on the cross when Jesus was crucified. The notice said, 'Jesus of Nazareth, King of the Jews', and it was written in Hebrew, Latin and Greek.

It seems likely that Jesus knew all four languages. Probably He spoke Aramaic and koine Greek, could read and write Hebrew, and knew a little Latin. There are countries today where it is normal for a person to know four languages. For example, an educated Muslim in Tanzania speaks his own tribal language, also Swahili (the *'lingua franca'* or common language used all over East Africa) and English, and he reads the Qur'an and says his prayers in Arabic.

STUDY SUGGESTIONS

WORDS AND MEANINGS

1. Explain the meaning of the words (a) 'recess' and (b) 'luxury' as used in this chapter.
2. What is meant by the 'official language' of a country?

REVIEW OF CONTENT

3. What sort of a town was Nazareth, and whereabouts in Palestine was it?
4. (a) What were the houses of ordinary people like in Palestine in Jesus's time? In what chief ways were they like or different from the sort of house you live in?
   (b) What sort of food did people mostly live on in Palestine in Jesus's time?
5. What sort of clothes did people wear in Palestine in Jesus's time? Which if any of the garments described are similar to garments worn by people in your own country today?
6. Describe the times and ways of praying that were and are customary among:
   (a) Jews   (b) Christians   (c) Muslims
   What do you see as the chief similarities and differences between them?
7. (a) For what reason did Jews keep the seventh day as a day of rest?
   (b) When does the Jewish sabbath begin, and when does it end?

(c) Where were Jews expected to go every sabbath?

(d) List three things that were forbidden for Jews on the sabbath.

8. (a) What was the usual way for a boy to learn a trade in Jesus's time?

(b) What was Jesus's trade?   (c) What was Paul's trade?

9. (a) What were the four languages used in Palestine in New Testament times?

(b) In which language was the New Testament written?

(c) What language did Jesus usually speak at home and among the ordinary people?

(d) What was the official language of the Roman Empire?

BIBLE STUDY

10. Read Matthew 27.39–46, Mark 15.29–34 and Psalm 22.1–11.

(a) Which verse of the psalm was Jesus quoting in His cry from the cross?

(b) As written down in the Jewish Scriptures the Psalms were in Hebrew, but according to the Gospel passages Jesus cried out the words of Psalm 22 in Aramaic. Why do you think He did so?

11. According to John 19.19–22, Pilate's notice about Jesus being the 'King of the Jews' was written in three languages. What were those languages, and which groups of people was each intended for?

FURTHER STUDY AND DISCUSSION

12. How many languages do you speak? What are the reasons for this? Which one do you prefer to use, and why?

13. Are the clergy in your Church paid by the Church, or do they have to earn all or part of their living by other means? What are the advantages and disadvantages of each system?

14. Why do some Christians call Sunday 'the sabbath'? Some people say there is no reason for Christians to apply Jewish rules about the sabbath to the Christian observance of Sunday. What is your opinion?

RELIGIOUS LIFE

THE TEMPLE AND SACRIFICE

'Day after day I sat in the temple' (Matt. 26.55). King Solomon built a Temple in Jerusalem more than 900 years before Jesus was born. The Temple was a house built for God. It was a place where God was especially present, and where His people could gather to worship Him.

The stone tablets with the Ten Commandments written on them were kept there in a wooden box called the Ark of the Covenant. The Ark was in the holiest part of the Temple, the 'Holy of Holies'. No one except the high priest was allowed to enter the Holy of Holies, and even he only did so once a year. There were altars in the Temple for sacrificing animals and for burning incense. Centuries before Jesus lived, the Jews had come to believe that the Temple was the only place where sacrifices could be made.

Every day, all through the year, priests and Levites offered worship to God through music, incense and sacrifice. Each year there were three great festivals: Passover, Pentecost, and Tabernacles (or Booths), when as many Jews as were able went to Jerusalem to worship the Lord.

Solomon's Temple stood for nearly 300 years. Then it was destroyed by invading armies. Most of the Temple treasures and thousands of Jewish people were taken away to Babylon. The Ark was probably destroyed at that time. Within a hundred years the Jews had returned and rebuilt the Temple. We call that Temple the second Temple. Not long before the birth of Jesus, King Herod the Great had rebuilt and extended the second Temple. When the Jews said to Jesus, 'it has taken 46 years to build this temple' (John 2.20), they were talking about Herod's Temple. See diagram, p. 11.

For Jesus and His followers the Temple was the centre of their religious life. Only priests were allowed to enter the sacred building itself, but the Temple was surrounded by several courtyards. In the New Testament the word 'Temple' nearly always means the courtyards, or Temple area. We can read in the Gospels about Jesus walking in the Temple and teaching there, 'by the treasury' and 'in the portico of Solomon' (Mark 12.41; John 8.20; 10.23). Jesus drove the traders and money-changers out of the Temple courtyard. The early Christians who lived in Jerusalem went to the Temple daily (Acts 2.46).

SYNAGOGUES AND THE LAW

'He went to the synagogue, as his custom was on the sabbath day' (Luke 4.16). The idea of the synagogue probably began when the Jews were living in Babylon and Solomon's Temple lay in ruins. Their traditional forms of worship had stopped, for sacrifices could only be made in the Temple itself. During the years in exile the Jews collected together and wrote down the traditions of their ancestors. What they wrote down became 'the Law', and those who studied and copied out the Law were 'scribes'. Jews began to gather in groups on the sabbath to hear the Law being read. This was the beginning of the synagogue, which really means a gathering. When special buildings were used for gathering and studying the law the buildings were also called synagogues.

Temple worship was centred on the offering of sacrifice. When the Temple was destroyed in AD 70, during the Jewish revolt against Roman Rule, Temple worship came to an end. Synagogue worship was centred on the reading of Scripture, and it continues to this day. Every sabbath, Jews meet together in synagogues to hear the Scriptures being read, translated and explained. A synagogue service can only take place when at least ten men are present. A boy is counted as a man when he is twelve or thirteen years old, and then he can take part in the reading. Jesus used to go to the synagogue on the sabbath. Sometimes He was invited to read the lesson and explain it (Luke 4.16–21). According to Acts it was also Paul's custom to attend the synagogue on the sabbath, and he was often invited to read and to preach (see Acts 17.2; 13.14).

PRIESTS AND SCRIBES

'Assembling the chief priests and the scribes of the people, Herod inquired of them where the Christ was to be born' (Matt. 2.4).

Priests: All Jewish priests had to be descendants of Aaron, the brother of Moses. Priests were trained in all the rituals of temple worship. They offered the sacrifices of animals and of incense. Zechariah, the father of John the Baptist, was a priest, and it was while he was offering the incense that the angel appeared and told him that John would be born (Luke 1.5–23).

Many of the priests were holy and devout men, like Zechariah. Some were really more interested in wealth, power and politics than in religion. Many belonged to a group known as the Sadducees (see below).

Scribes: A scribe is a person whose job is to write things down. The Jewish scribes not only copied out the Law, but spent their lives studying it. They became experts in the Law, knowing and understanding it, and interpreting its meaning to others. In the New Testament the word 'scribe' is always used in this way, meaning someone who was an expert in the Jewish law. Luke sometimes calls the scribes 'lawyers'. Many of the scribes belonged to a group called Pharisees ('And some of the scribes of the Pharisees' party stood up' Acts 23.9).

PHARISEES AND SADDUCEES

'When Paul perceived that one part were Sadducees and the other Pharisees, he cried out in the council, "Brethren, I am a Pharisee, a son of Pharisees; with respect to the hope and resurrection of the dead I am on trial." And when he had said this, a dissension arose between the Pharisees and Sadducees; and the assembly was divided. For the Sadducees say that there is no resurrection, nor angel, nor spirit; but the Pharisees acknowledge them all' (Acts 23.6–8).

'When special buildings were used for gathering to read the Law they were called synagogues.' These synagogue ruins at Capernaum date from the 3rd or 4th century AD, but some archaeologists think they may stand on the same site as the earlier synagogue building where Jesus taught.

The Sanhedrin or Council which met at Jerusalem was the highest Jewish lawcourt. When Jesus was arrested He was taken to the Sanhedrin (as were Peter, John, Stephen and Paul). The chief Rabbinical Court in Jerusalem is the modern equivalent, where cases relating to Jewish religious law are held today.

Sadducees: The Sadducees were priests. They were very conservative in their religious beliefs. They only accepted the Law of Moses as being Scripture. They did not believe in angels, nor that human beings have a soul, nor that there is another life after this one.

Pharisees: Unlike the Sadducees, the Pharisees believed that the Law could be developed. They accepted an oral law as well as the written law. The Pharisees tried to keep the Law in every detail. They also taught it to others, especially in the synagogues and schools. They believed in a resurrection and a life after death, as well as in angels and demons. However, they also believed that only those people who kept the Law in every detail would be raised at the resurrection. Paul was a Pharisee, and had been trained in the Jewish Law.

THE TRADITIONS OF THE ELDERS

'The Pharisees and the scribes asked him, "Why do your disciples not live according to the traditions of the elders, but eat with hands defiled?"' (Mark 7.5). For several centuries before Jesus lived the Torah had been interpreted by the scribes. They used a method called '*midrash*' to find and teach the deeper meaning of the Scriptures. Their interpretation of the written law was passed on by word of mouth from one generation to the next. The Pharisees called this oral law '*the traditions of the elders*'. They believed that God had given it to Moses on Mount Sinai at the same time as He gave the Torah.

At the end of the 2nd century AD the oral law was collected and written down, and was called the '*Mishnah*'. Later still the rabbis' discussions of the Mishnah were written down and called the '*Gemara*'. The Mishnah and Gemara together form the '*Talmud*'. Jews still consider the Talmud to be an authoritative guide to the spiritual life, second only to the Scriptures themselves.

THE SANHEDRIN

'Now the chief priests and the whole council sought testimony against Jesus to put him to death' (Mark 14.55). The Sanhedrin was the Jewish council which met in Jerusalem, and had the high priest as its president. Originally all the members of the Sanhedrin had been Sadducees, but by the time Jesus lived there were also many Pharisees in it. It was the highest Jewish court, and even under the Romans it had great power. When Jesus was arrested He was taken first to the Sanhedrin. 'The assembly of the elders of the people gathered together, both chief priests and scribes; and they led him away to their council' (Luke 22.66). Stephen also was taken before the council. So were Peter and John and Paul. Paul being a former Pharisee himself, caused a division of opinion in the council when he was put on trial (Acts 23.6–8, see p. 17).

ESSENES

The Essenes were a Jewish sect which probably began about 150 years before the birth of Jesus. They were the followers of someone whom they called 'the Teacher of Righteousness'. Essenes considered that the rest of Judaism was corrupt and wicked, and so they kept themselves apart. A large group of them lived a monastic life by the Dead Sea, at a place called Qumran. They spent a lot of time studying and interpreting the Scriptures. The Dead Sea Scrolls are a collection of their writings which were first discovered in 1947. The community at Qumran shared all their income and property. Other Essenes lived in towns and villages, and kept their own money, but still lived apart from other people as far as possible.

Essenes are not mentioned in the New Testament, but Josephus, a Jewish historian who wrote in the first century AD, names them as one of the three religious groups of Judaism. We know a lot about the Qumran Community from the Dead Sea Scrolls. Possibly the Essenes had an influence on John the Baptist and Jesus.

THE HOPE FOR A MESSIAH

The Jews were expecting God to send them a Messiah. 'Messiah' is a Hebrew word meaning someone who is anointed. 'Christ' is the Greek word which means the same thing. The Israelite kings had been anointed king. The high priest was also anointed when he took office. Anointing had to do with being set apart and being given power. In the time of Jesus the Jews were waiting for God to send them a powerful deliverer.

Most Jews expected the Messiah to be a political leader, a king who would be a descendant of King David. They thought that he would lead an army against the Romans and defeat them. Then he would establish a Jewish kingdom. He would celebrate the establishment of his kingdom with a great banquet. The kingdom of the Messiah would be as great and powerful as the kingdom of Israel had been in the days of David. All the scattered Jews would return to live in Israel. The Messiah would be a righteous king and judge. His subjects would live in peace and prosperity. There would be plenty of food and drink for everyone, and even the animals would live in peace. Everyone would know God and worship Him.

Some Jews had a more spiritual idea of what the Messiah would be like. For example, the Essenes seem to have expected three people: a prophet like Moses who would lead them into all truth, a warrior Messiah who would be descended from David, and a priestly Messiah, descended from Aaron. The most important of these was the priestly Messiah. The Samaritans were expecting a prophet like Moses (see pp. 24–26).

STUDY SUGGESTIONS

WORDS AND MEANINGS

1. What do the words 'Messiah' and 'Christ' mean, and what language does each come from?
2. What is 'incense'?
3. Explain the meaning of 'conservative', as used in the phrase 'conservative in their beliefs' (p. 19). Suggest a word to describe a person who is the *opposite* of conservative in his religious beliefs.
4. Match each of the Jewish terms (a)–(e) with the definition from (f)–(j) below which belongs to it.
   (a) Torah   (b) Gemara   (c) Midrash   (d) Mishnah
   (e) Talmud
   (f) A collection of Jewish oral law, not written down until early in the 3rd century AD.
   (g) A method of interpreting the Scriptures and teaching the oral law, in use long before the time of Jesus.
   (h) The written Law of the Jews, believed to have been given to Moses on Mount Sinai.
   (i) The discussions of the Mishnah by the rabbis, later written down.
   (j) A combination of the Mishnah and the Gemara.
5. What is usually meant by 'monastic'? What sort of life is it used to describe in this chapter?

REVIEW OF CONTENT

6. (a) Who built the first Temple in Jerusalem?
   (b) What was the 'Holy of Holies', and what important object was kept there?
   (c) Why was the Temple of Jesus's time called 'Herod's Temple'?
   (d) What activity could only be carried out in the Temple, and nowhere else?
   (e) Who was allowed into the Temple building itself?
7. What does the word 'synagogue' mean, and what is the main purpose of a synagogue?
8. In Jewish religion: (a) Who was able to be a priest?   (b) What was a priest's job?
9. What were Jewish lawyers called and what did their work consist of?
10. What was the Sanhedrin, and who were members of it?
11. How is it that we know a lot about the Essenes, although the New Testament does not mention them?

BIBLE STUDY

12. Read Luke 1.5–23. What can we learn from this story of Zechariah

21

about the duties of a priest and the way in which the duties were organized?
13. Read Mark 12.18–23. What does this passage tell us about the Sadducees?
14. Read Matt. 9.14 and Mark 7.3. What do these two passages teach us about how the Pharisees lived?
15. Which people, or groups of people, were anointed, and for what purpose, according to each of the following verses?
(a) 1 Sam. 24.10   (b) Lev. 16.32   (c) Acts 4.27   (d) Isa. 45.1
(e) Heb. 1.9   (f) 1 John 2.27   (g) James 5.14.

FURTHER STUDY AND DISCUSSION

16. Find out more about the three great Jewish festivals, Passover, Pentecost, and Tabernacles. What does each celebrate and at what time of year is it held? What Christian festivals are held at similar times, and why?
17. Find out more about the Essenes who lived at Qumran, and then write as full a description as you can of the way they lived.
18. Anointing is still used in various Churches to symbolize a person being set apart and given power. If you are not familiar with the practice, find out who does it, when, and why. What other ways do you know of by which people may be set apart?
19. Pharisees and Sadducees differed from each other as to which aspects of the Jewish religion they thought most important and valued most. Give some examples of groups within the Christian Church who differ from others as to what aspects of Christianity they value most. Which aspects are the most frequent causes of disagreement? What religion, if any, do you know of in which there are *no* differences of opinion or practice between different groups?

SOME MATTERS OF HISTORY

'Jesus was born . . . in the days of Herod the King' (Matt. 2.1).

ROMAN RULE

In the century before Jesus was born the Romans had taken control of Palestine and made it a part of their empire. Judaea, Samaria and Galilee were all part of the Roman Province of Syria (see map, p. x). The Romans were not a very religious people. They were good administrators, anxious to have a well organized and peaceful empire. They usually allowed the different nations which they ruled to follow their own religion. Judaism was a *'religio licita'* (Latin for 'legally permitted religion'), and the Romans made allowances for the Jewish religious beliefs (e.g. Jews were not expected to offer sacrifices to Roman gods). The Sanhedrin was allowed to have power, especially in religious matters. When the Jewish leaders took Jesus to Pilate he said, 'Take him yourselves, and judge him by your own law' (John 18.31).

HEROD THE GREAT

The Romans ruled much of their conquered territory through the local kings and chiefs. In 40 BC they appointed Herod, later called Herod the Great, to be King of Judaea. Herod's ancestors were Edomites. He was only half a Jew, and he was a friend of the Romans, so that many Jews hated him. He did a great deal of building during his reign. He built cities, palaces and fortresses, and rebuilt the Temple. He was a strong and clever king, also a cruel one. He did not hesitate to have members of his own family killed in order to protect his power. Herod the Great is the Herod who is mentioned in the stories about the birth of Jesus (e.g. Matt. 2.1; Luke 1.5). He was just the sort of man to order that all the baby boys in Bethlehem should be killed.

HEROD'S SONS

After Herod the Great died in 4 BC his territory was divided between three of his sons. Philip ruled the northern and north-eastern parts, and ruled in peace until he died in AD 33. Herod Antipas ruled Galilee until AD 39. Archelaus ruled Judaea and Samaria. Archelaus was such a bad ruler that the Jews begged the Romans to remove him, and they agreed. From AD 6 Judaea and Samaria were ruled by Roman prefects, who were later given the title of 'procurator'. Pontius Pilate was prefect from about AD 26–36.

All these people are mentioned in the Gospel stories. Herod Antipas is the Herod who appears most often. It was Herod Antipas who married his brother's wife, who imprisoned John the Baptist and then beheaded him (Mark 6.14–29). Jesus described Herod as 'that fox', and warned His disciples to beware 'the leaven of Herod' (Luke 13.31; Mark 8.15). Herod Antipas and Pilate are both mentioned in Acts as well (Acts 4.27).

HEROD AGRIPPA

A third Herod who appears in the New Testament was a grandson of Herod the Great and a nephew of Herod Antipas. He came to be known as Herod Agrippa. He grew up in Rome, and by AD 41 he had been made ruler of the whole of his grandfather's kingdom. He was popular with the Jews, and it seems that he tried to increase his popularity by attacking the early Christians. It was Herod Agrippa who killed James the son of Zebedee and put Peter in prison. His death is described in Acts 12.2–3, 20–23.

HEROD AGRIPPA II

When Herod Agrippa died his son, also called Agrippa, was a lad of only seventeen. As he grew older the Romans gradually gave him more areas of Palestine to rule over, and he became Herod Agrippa II. This is the Agrippa before whom Paul appeared (Acts 25.13–26.32). Bernice who was with Agrippa was his sister, and another of his sisters, Drusilla, was married to the Roman prefect Felix (Acts 24.24).

THE JEWISH WAR AND THE FALL OF JERUSALEM

Agrippa II was not a strong king like his great-grandfather. The Roman prefects who were sent to govern Palestine became less and less sympathetic to the Jews. Often they failed to respect Jewish customs and beliefs, and the taxes were heavy. The tension between the Jews and their Roman rulers increased each year, until finally the Jews could endure no more and rebelled. The Jewish War broke out in AD 66, and it took the Romans seven years before they defeated the last Jewish stronghold. The Jews suffered terribly in the war. In AD 70 the city of Jerusalem was captured after a long siege, and the Temple was destroyed. The whole city was destroyed except for three towers of Herod the Great's palace and a small part of the city wall.

ANOTHER REBELLION

In spite of the suffering they had endured during the Jewish War, the Jews rebelled again about sixty years later. That rebellion is known as the Revolt of Bar Cocheba, and it lasted for three years. After that the Romans built a Roman city on the site of Jerusalem. Where the Temple had stood they build a Temple to the Roman god Jupiter. No Jew was allowed to set foot in the city except on one day in the year. Even the name of Judaea, meaning the land of the Jews, was changed. It was called Palestine, meaning the land of the Philistines.

After these events Judaism became more and more a religion of the Law. The Temple and its sacrifices had been swept away. The Sanhedrin had gone. There was no work for priests or Sadducees. The Jews gathered around the Law, and the teachers of the Law became their leaders.

SAMARITANS

The Samaritans were the inhabitants of Samaria, the country which lay between Galilee and Judaea. By ancestry and by religion they were closely related to the Jews. The Samaritans were descended from the northern tribes of Israel who had inter-married with people from other countries many centuries before Jesus lived. The Samaritans had the law of Moses, but sometimes interpreted it differently, e.g. they believed that the holy place where sacrifice was to be offered was on

24

In AD 70 the city of Jerusalem was taken, after a Jewish uprising, by the Romans under Titus who later became Emperor, and the Temple was destroyed. The triumphal arch in Rome commemorating Titus's victory shows the soldiers looting the Temple and carrying away the golden lampstand and table, and the silver trumpets and other sacred treasures.

Mount Gerizim, not in the Temple on Mount Zion (see John 4.20).

For centuries the Jews and Samaritans had been increasingly hostile to each other. The Jews despised the Samaritans, considering that they were hardly better than non-Jews. The Samaritans resented the attitude taken by the Jews. In Jesus's day Jews and Samaritans hated each other. The quickest route from Galilee to Jerusalem was through Samaria, but many Jews chose to go the long way round rather than travel through Samaria.

STUDY SUGGESTIONS

WORDS AND MEANINGS

1. Find another way of saying: 'The Romans made allowances for Jewish religious beliefs'.
2. Find out the original meaning of 'popular'. What does the word generally mean today?

REVIEW OF CONTENT

3. Judaea was part of which Roman Province?
4. What was a *religio licita*? What privileges did the Jews have on account of Judaism being a *religio licita*?
5. Why did many Jews hate Herod the Great?
6. (a) In which year was the Temple in Jerusalem destroyed by a Roman army?
   (b) What did the Romans later build on the site of the Jerusalem Temple?
7. What is the original meaning of the name Palestine?
8. Explain briefly who was each of the following:
   (a) Pontius Pilate (b) Archelaus (c) Agrippa (see Acts 26)
   (d) Bernice (e) Drusilla (f) Felix

BIBLE STUDY

9. Which Herod is referred to in each of the following verses?
   (a) Matt. 2.19 (b) Luke 9.7 (c) Luke 23.7 (d) Acts 12.1.
10. Use a concordance to find as many references as you can to centurions. From these references, what sort of men do they seem to have been?
11. Read Luke 9.51–56; John 4.4–9; 8.48. What do these verses tell us about the feelings which Jews and Samaritans had for each other?

FURTHER STUDY AND DISCUSSION

12. The Romans 'permitted' most religions to be practised within their Empire. What religions are 'permitted' in your country?

How far and for what reasons do you think it is a good idea for governments to be tolerant of different religious beliefs and practices?

13. Most governments, even 'totalitarian' ones, have a need to be 'popular'. In what ways does the government of your country try to win popularity, and for what reasons?

14. Some Jews called Jesus a 'Samaritan' when they wanted to insult Him. Yet nowadays to call a person a Samaritan is generally a compliment. Why do you think this change has come about?
Because of the change in the meaning of 'Samaritan' Jesus's story has lost a lot of its original meaning. Rewrite the story of the Good Samaritan in a way that will restore its meaning for people in your country today.

15. Find out as much as you can about Bar Cocheba and the revolt that bears his name.
In what circumstances, if any, do you think it is right for a Christian to become a 'freedom fighter'? (It has been said that 'One party's "freedom-fighter" is the opposing party's "terrorist".' What is your opinion?)

Special Note A: Dates

When we say that Herod Antipas was tetrarch of Galilee from 4 BC until AD 39 we are using the Christian calendar, which was not invented until the 6th century AD. There are no dates of this sort anywhere in the New Testament. The only way in which 1st century writers could give a date was by referring to some other event. The Romans often dated an event by saying that it occurred so many years after the foundation of the city of Rome. Luke used a similar method to give the year when John the Baptist began to preach: 'In the fifteenth year of the reign of Tiberius Caesar, Pontius Pilate being Governor of Judaea, and Herod being tetrarch of Galilee, and his brother Philip being tetrarch of the region of Ituraea and Trachonitis, and Lysanias tetrarch of Abilene, in the highpriesthood of Annas and Caiaphas, the word of God came to John' (Luke 3.1–2).

The Christian calendar was worked out by a monk called Dionysius Exiguus. He dated everything from the birth of Jesus. The years that follow the birth of Jesus are called Anno Domini (AD) meaning 'in the year of our Lord' (e.g. we would say that John the Baptist began to preach in AD 27). All the years before the birth of Christ are called BC: 'Before Christ'. These dates seem to be counted backwards, e.g. the Jewish Exile was from 587–538 BC. This is because the beginning of the Exile was more years 'before Christ' than the end of the Exile.

If we look up the dates when Jesus lived in a modern encyclopedia we find them given as 5 BC–AD 30 (or sometimes 6 BC–AD 29). These dates are very confusing. It seems that Dionysius, or Dennis the Little as we would call him in English, made some mistakes in his mathematics when working out his calendar. Herod the Great died in the year which we now call 4 BC. Since he was ruler of Palestine when Jesus was born, we deduce a date of 5 or 6 BC for the year of Jesus's birth.

Muslims have a completely different calendar, since they count their years from the Hijra, when Muhammad emigrated from Mecca to Medina. According to the Christian calendar the Hijra took place in the year AD 622. In the Muslim calendar AD 1986 is 1406 AH. We also find the letters CE used in place of AD, and BCE in place of BC. CE stands for Common Era, BCE stands for Before Common Era.

Dionysius Exiguus's own dates are given as AD 500–550. This can also be expressed as 'early sixth century AD'. This may look confusing, but is actually logical. All years from 1 to 100 are in the 1st century. Years from 101 to 200 are in the 2nd century, and so on.

STUDY SUGGESTIONS

WORDS AND MEANINGS

1. What is the meaning of 'deduce', as in the sentence 'we deduce a date of 5 or 6 BC for the birth of Jesus'?

REVIEW OF CONTENT

2. In what way did the Romans often give a date to an event?
3. Who invented the Christian calendar, and in which century did he do it?
4. In which century was the year AD 314?

BIBLE STUDY

5. Look up 1 Kings 15.1, 9, 25, 33. What method did the writer of Kings use to show the year when each king began to reign?

FURTHER STUDY AND DISCUSSION

6. The Oxford Dictionary of the Christian Church gives the dates '*c*.37–*c*.100' for the Jewish historian Josephus. What does the '*c*.' mean in each case, and why is it used? In what way could your answer to this question affect your study and use of Josephus's work?
7. Literature from the State of Israel uses CE and BCE rather than AD and BC when giving dates. Why do you think that is so? Which other countries would you expect to use CE and BCE, and for what reasons?
8. Imagine that one of your friends is very confused because he has discovered that Jesus was apparently born 'before Christ'. Write a paragraph to explain the matter to him.

3

Jesus the Teacher

TEACHER AND DISCIPLES

'Rabbi, we know that you are a teacher come from God' (John 3.2).

JEWISH TEACHERS

Jesus was probably about thirty years old when He left His home and work to become a teacher. The Hebrew word 'rabbi' means literally 'my great one', and it came to mean a teacher. Today Jewish teachers are still called 'Rabbi'. In the Gospels we often read that people called Jesus 'Rabbi' or 'Teacher'.

When Jesus became a teacher He collected a group of followers, or 'disciples', and began to wander around the country, teaching His disciples and anyone else who wanted to listen. Other teachers did the same. Jesus's cousin, John the Baptist, was also a teacher and had disciples: 'The disciples of John told him of all these things. And John, calling to him two of his disciples, sent them to the Lord' (Luke 7.18). John also moved about from place to place, although in his case he had to go where there was water in order to baptize people.

There was one unusual thing about Jesus as a teacher. Most people became a teacher after first being the disciple of another teacher. As far as we know Jesus had never been a disciple of anyone else. People found this strange: 'About the middle of the feast Jesus went up into the temple and taught. The Jews marvelled at it, saying, "How is it that this man has learning when he has never studied?"' (John 7.14–15).

JESUS'S MINISTRY

The time which Jesus spent travelling around Palestine as a teacher is generally called His 'ministry', which means 'service'. Jesus's ministry was spent in serving people by preaching, teaching and healing them. He mixed with all sorts of people. Some of His friends were rich and powerful, but most of them were ordinary working people. Crowds came to hear Jesus speak: 'And he left there and went to the region of Judaea and beyond the Jordan, and crowds gathered to him again; and again, as his custom was, he taught them' (Mark 10.1).

As news spread that Jesus could work miracles people came from all over the place. They came to be healed themselves, or to bring sick friends and relatives. Some came out of curiosity, to see what He would do next. 'And a multitude followed him, because they saw the signs which he did on those who were diseased' (John 6.2).

JESUS' DISCIPLES

Out of the crowds who went to listen to Jesus some were convinced that He was sent from God, and became disciples. Not all the people who believed in Him travelled around with Him. Nevertheless they can be called His disciples.

Secret Disciples: 'Joseph of Arimathea, who was a disciple of Jesus, but secretly, for fear of the Jews' (John 19.38). Some of the people who met Jesus became 'secret disciples'. They did not admit openly to being followers of Jesus. Nicodemus and Joseph of Arimathea were both secret disciples. They were wealthy men in high positions, who might have had a lot of difficulty if their support for Him became known. Probably neither of them ever considered wandering around the country with Jesus. Nicodemus supported Jesus in a meeting of the Sanhedrin, and supplied an enormous quantity of spices to anoint His body. Joseph of Arimathea got Pilate's permission to take Jesus' body from the cross, and provided a newly cut tomb (Mark 15.42–46; John 7.50; 19.39).

Women Disciples: 'Soon afterwards he went on through cities and villages, preaching and bringing the good news of the kingdom of God. And the twelve were with him, and also some women who had been healed of evil spirits and infirmities: Mary, called Magdalene, from whom seven demons had gone out, and Joanna, the wife of Chuza, Herod's steward, and Susanna, and many others, who provided for them out of their means' (Luke 8.1–3). We do not know how many women became disciples. Luke names three of them, and states that there were 'many others'. He says that some of them were women whom Jesus had healed, but gives no other details except in the case of Mary Magdalene. From this passage it appears that on some occasions the women travelled with Jesus. They also 'provided out of their means'. This suggests money and other practical help. Jesus and the disciples who travelled with Him shared their money, but since they had given up their jobs, they depended on other people for everything.

Jesus enjoyed the warmth and comfort of His friends' homes. When He went to Jerusalem He liked to stay with His friends, Martha, Mary and Lazarus. In Peter's house his mother-in-law 'served Jesus and his disciples'. That may only mean that she served a meal, but might also mean that she became a follower of Jesus.

Some of the women disciples showed great courage in their following. They were the ones who remained near Jesus throughout the crucifixion, and they were the first to visit the tomb on Sunday morning (see Luke 23.27, 55).

Non-travelling Disciples: 'The man who had been possessed with demons begged him that he might be with him. But he refused, and said to him, "Go home to your friends and tell them how much the Lord has done for you"' (Mark 5.18–19). Some of Jesus's followers stayed at home, e.g. the demon-possessed man at Gerasa. Probably most of the women disciples stayed at home. We only read of Jesus meeting with Martha and Mary in Bethany. Another disciple in Bethany was Simon the Leper (Mark 14.3). Probably Simon was someone else whom Jesus had healed. What is certain is that he no longer had leprosy. If he had still been a leper, he could not have lived in the village, or entertained people in his home.

Temporary Disciples: 'After this many of his disciples drew back and no longer went about with him' (John 6.66). There was a time in Jesus's ministry when He had so many disciples travelling about with Him that He was able to send seventy of them on a mission. He sent the disciples out in pairs to go into towns and villages to preach and heal (Luke 10.1–17). Some of the seventy may not have remained faithful. We do not hear again of so many disciples being involved in Jesus's ministry in Palestine. Popular support for Jesus declined when people realized that He was not going to be the political Messiah they were hoping for (see p. 20).

THE TWELVE

'He appointed twelve, to be with him, and to be sent out to preach and have authority to cast out demons' (Mark 3.14–15). From out of Jesus's many disciples He chose twelve 'to be with him'. These twelve were all men, and they all left their homes and travelled about with Jesus. They stayed with Jesus all through His ministry. Later they (and some others) came to be called 'apostles', or messengers (see Glossary), because He had sent them out to carry God's word into the world (John 20.21).

The New Testament contains three lists of the names of the Twelve, and these lists are not exactly the same (see Matt. 10.2–4; Mark 3.16–19; Luke 6.14–16). Perhaps some of the Twelve had more than one name. Several of them are not mentioned anywhere else, so that we know nothing more about them. Others we do know more about, and from them we can see that Jesus chose a group of people who were very different from each other.

FOUR FISHERMEN

At least four of the Twelve were fishermen. One of these was Andrew, who had also been a follower of John the Baptist. According to John's Gospel he became a disciple because of what he heard John the Baptist say about Jesus (John 1.35–40). We generally remember Andrew for the way he introduced other people to Jesus. One of the people he introduced was his brother Simon, also a fisherman.

Jesus gave Simon a nickname, 'The Rock', 'Rocky'. In Hebrew it is

From His many disciples Jesus chose twelve to be with Him and to preach and cast out demons. At least four of them were fishermen, accustomed to an outdoor life of hardship and danger, as fishermen on Lake Galilee still are. All who accept God's call to be disciples of Jesus – as these candidates for the ministry in Madagascar and their college tutors have done – must have 'zeal' enough to accept that some hardships may lie ahead.

Cephas, in Greek it is Petros, so we call him Peter. In the Gospel of John and the letters of Paul he is sometimes called Cephas. Of all the Twelve Peter is the one we know the most about: e.g. we know that he lived in Capernaum, that he was married, that he was an impetuous man who was often the first person to act or speak. Peter is also one of the leading personalities in the Book of Acts.

Two more fishermen were James and John the sons of Zebedee. These brothers helped their father in the family fishing business, a business which was big enough to use paid workers (Mark 1.20). Jesus gave them a nickname too. He called them Boanerges, 'sons of thunder'. James and John may also have been Jesus's relations. Some people think that their mother Salome was a cousin of Mary, Jesus's mother.

A TAX-COLLECTOR

Matthew, who was also called Levi, was a tax-collector for the Romans before Jesus chose him as one of the Twelve. The Jews hated tax-collectors for two reasons: (1) they were helping the hated Roman rulers; (2) many tax-collectors were corrupt, and used their official position to get rich quickly. We do not know whether Matthew had been corrupt, but we do know that his friends were other 'tax-collectors and sinners'. No respectable person would be the friend of a tax-collector. When Matthew gave a party for Jesus and His disciples, he invited his friends, and the scribes and Pharisees were shocked (Matt. 9.9–11; Mark 2.13–17).

A ZEALOT

Two of the Twelve were called Simon. As well as Simon nicknamed Peter there was Simon the Zealot, also called Simon the Cananean. The Zealots were a group of Jews who were even more nationalistic than their fellows, and had an even deeper hatred of the Romans. They were revolutionaries, freedom fighters. They expected God to give His people a political kingdom, and they were ready to use violence in order to support it. They did not want power for themselves. They were full of zeal for God and for His kingdom. Simon the Zealot and Matthew the tax-collector must have found it very strange that Jesus could choose both of them to be in the Twelve.

MARRIED MEN

The only one of the twelve whom we know for certain to have been married is Peter, but probably all the Twelve were married (see e.g. Mark 10.29–30; Luke 18.28–30). As far as we know Jesus never married, but it was very unusual for a Jewish man not to marry. Nearly all the rabbis had wives.

THE THREE

Among the Twelve there were three disciples who were especially close to Jesus. On several occasions we read that Jesus just took three disciples with Him: Peter, James and John. He took these three when He went with Jairus to his house (Mark 5.37). He took them when He went up the mountain and was transfigured (Mark 9.2). He took the same three on one side in the garden on the night before the crucifixion and begged them to watch and pray (Mark 14.32–34).

STUDY SUGGESTIONS

WORDS AND MEANINGS

1. What do the following words mean?
   (a) 'apostle'   (b) 'rabbi'   (c) 'zealot'?
2. Look up the verb 'to minister' in a dictionary. Which of the meanings given could be applied to the ministry of Jesus?
3. A 'disciple' is one who follows. What are some of the ways in which it is possible to 'follow' someone?

REVIEW OF CONTENT

4. Suggest (a) two ways in which Jesus was like other Jewish teachers, and (b) two ways in which Jesus was *un*like most other Jewish teachers.
5. List three different trades or occupations followed by members of the Twelve before they followed Jesus.
6. Which of the following disciples travelled with Jesus, as far as we know?
   (a) Andrew   (b) Lazarus   (c) Simon the leper   (d) Nicodemus
   (e) Mary Magdalene   (f) Matthew

BIBLE STUDY

7. Read Matthew 4.18; Mark 1.29–31; Luke 4.38–39; 5.1–11. What do we learn from these verses about Peter's background and family life?
8. Read Mark 10.29–31. What was Jesus saying that His followers had left for the sake of the Kingdom of God? What do these verses imply about the people He was speaking to?
9. Luke mentions Mary Magdalene, Joanna and Susanna as disciples of Jesus. Use a concordance to find the references to these women, and say what information is given about each.
10. Read the parable of the Sower (Mark 4.1–20). What does this parable teach us about the reasons why some disciples *give up* following?

FURTHER STUDY AND DISCUSSION

11. 'To be with him, and to be sent out to preach and have authority to cast out demons' (Mark 3.14–15). It was for these three purposes that Jesus chose the Twelve disciples.
Which of the three do you consider the most important? How far does the Church expect (a) its ordained leaders, and (b) ordinary lay Christians, to carry out these purposes today?

12. Jesus spoke about the cost of becoming His disciple (Luke 14.26–33). What, if any, is the cost to *you*, or to others in your community, of being a follower of Jesus?

13. When Jesus chose the Twelve He included people of opposing political views. What examples are there in your country of Christians holding opposing political views? How far do you think that being members of the Church can help to unite people from the different groups?

14. In many countries there are people who say that the Church should not meddle in politics, but stick to 'saving souls'. There are other people who say that it is the duty of the Church to give a lead in politics. What is your opinion?

JESUS' TEACHING METHODS

Jesus taught all His followers. He taught anyone who was willing to listen, but those whom He taught the most were the Twelve. Sometimes He taught them along with great crowds of other followers. At other times He took them away to lonely places, so that He could teach them on their own. Jesus was careful to teach them in such a way that they would remember what He had said.

Jesus had none of the equipment which modern teachers use. He did not even have a blackboard. In those days a teacher spoke, and his disciples were expected to remember what he had said. Jesus' disciples were used to learning things by heart, so it was probably easier for them than it would be for most of us. Yet it was still true that the more skilful the teacher was, the more easily his disciples were able to remember what he had taught them.

PARABLES AND ALLEGORY

'He taught them many things in parables' (Mark 4.2).

1. *Parables*: We may describe a parable as a story or a picture which teaches. Most people think of parables as stories, and Jesus told many stories. Some of them are long stories, e.g. the Good Samaritan, the Prodigal Son, the Labourers in the Vineyard (Luke 10.30–37; 15.11–32; Matt. 20.1–16). Others are very short stories, such as the ones about the

Wise Man and the Foolish Man, and the Lost Sheep (Matt. 7.24–27; Luke 15.4–7).

Jesus also used 'picture-language' without actually telling a story at all. Here are two 'pictures' which the Gospel writers call 'parables':

'He also told them a parable: "Can a blind man lead a blind man? Will they both not fall into a pit?"' (Luke 6.39).

'He told them another parable. "The kingdom of heaven is like leaven which a woman took and hid in three measures of meal, till it was all leavened"' (Matt. 13.33).

A parable may be a story, or it may be just a picture, told in order to teach something.

In its original context a parable was intended to teach one central truth. So the parable of the Good Samaritan teaches the truth that the neighbour we should love is anyone with whom we come into contact, and that compassion takes no account of human divisions. The parable of the Lost Sheep shows us the seeking, searching love of God. In some parables it is difficult to work out what was the central truth that Jesus wanted to teach.

The Hebrew word meaning 'parable' is '*mashal*', which also means a riddle. Parables are also riddles, things which stick in the mind, to be puzzled over. Jesus's disciples often found them puzzling: 'And when they were alone, those who were about him with the twelve asked him concerning the parables' (Mark 4.10).

2. *Allegory*: Allegory is related to parable, but different. In a parable there is a central truth, but in an allegory every detail is important. When Jesus used the picture of the vine (John 15.1–6) He was using an allegory. He stated that He was the vine, His Father was the vine-dresser, and the disciples were the branches. Vines and vineyards are often used as symbols of Israel in the Old Testament (see e.g. Hos. 10.1).

Another allegory that Jesus told was the story of the wicked tenants (Mark 12.1–10). In that story a man planted a vineyard and let it to tenants. When he sent his servants to get some fruit from the vineyard the tenants sent them away, and even beat and killed some of them. Finally the owner sent his own son, and the tenants killed him. Because Jesus was using an allegory from the Old Testament the Jewish leaders understood its meaning and tried to arrest Jesus. They knew He meant that the owner of the vineyard was God and they themselves were the tenants.

In practice it is sometimes difficult to know whether Jesus was using a parable or an allegory. The parable of the Sower (Matt. 13.3–9; Mark 4.3–9; Luke 8.5–8) is often treated as an allegory, and Jesus Himself is said to have explained the details to His disciples. However a number of scholars believe that Jesus first told it as a parable, teaching the central

truth that the kingdom of God would grow and produce a rich harvest
in spite of setbacks and disappointments.

ILLUSTRATIONS FROM EVERYDAY LIFE

'Look at the birds of the air ... consider the lilies of the field' (Matt.
6.26, 28). Jesus took His stories and pictures from the everyday world
around Him. He told stories about farmers and shepherds, travellers
and merchants, judges and rulers, weddings and unexpected visitors,
masters and servants, fathers and sons. He took the things of everyday
life and gave them a new significance. For example, Jesus told a story
about a shepherd searching for a lost sheep, and a woman hunting all
through the house for a lost coin. He made it clear that their joy when
they found what was lost was like God's joy when one sinner repented
(Luke 15.3–10). When Jesus wanted to show that to follow Him would
be costly He talked about two people: a builder who does not start to
build until he knows that he has enough money to finish the job, and a
king who does not go to war unless he knows he has some chance of
winning (Luke 14.27–33). Jesus constantly illustrated His teaching with
pictures from nature, speaking of sparrows and foxes, fig trees and
vines, thorns and thistles, bread, wineskins, doors ... and many more.

HUMOUR

'Can a blind man lead a blind man? Will they not both fall into a pit?'
(Luke 6.39). The people who first listened to Jesus must often have
laughed at the pictures He drew for them. Today we may miss the
humour in what He said, for two main reasons:

1. *Cultural differences*: Humour varies greatly from culture to culture. Moreover, things that were common to Jesus's hearers may be
unknown to us. Jesus's parable about blind guides is still amusing in
countries where every blind man has a small boy to be his guide.

2. *Familiarity*: Even the funniest story stops being funny when it has
been heard too often. For this reason the humour in many of Jesus's
sayings has been forgotten. Consider how the following may have once
caused people to smile:

'Why do you see the speck that is in your brother's eye, but do not
notice the log that is in your own eye? Or how can you say to your
brother, "Let me take the speck out of your eye," when there is the log
in your own eye?' (Matt. 7.3–4). 'No one after lighting a lamp puts it in
a cellar or under a bushel' (Luke 11.33).

EXAGGERATION

'It is easier for a camel to go through the eye of a needle than for a rich
man to enter the kingdom of God' (Mark 10.25). The idea of a camel
getting through the eye of a needle is a joke. It is also exaggerated, or

overstated. Jesus appeared to be saying that it was completely impossible for a rich person to enter the kingdom of heaven. Mark goes on to say that the disciples 'were exceedingly astonished', and Jesus reassured them that 'with men it is impossible, but not with God'.

Jesus was exaggerating, putting His point across very strongly in order to make people wake up and take notice. Preachers and teachers often say things to startle their listeners. Consider also this saying: 'If anyone comes to me and does not hate his own father and mother and wife and children and brothers and sisters, yes, and even his own life, he cannot be my disciple' (Luke 14.26).

PARADOX

'If anyone would be first, he must be last of all and servant of all' (Mark 9.35). This statement seems absurd when we first hear it. A statement such as this, which seems to contradict itself, is called a paradox. Paradox is most often used when we are dealing with mysterious things which we do not clearly understand. Christian doctrine about the nature of God is full of paradoxes.

Paradox was one of the methods which Jesus used to try to explain the kingdom of God. God's kingdom as Jesus described it is quite different from the kingdoms of the world. For example, in God's kingdom the servants are the most important people (Mark 9.35), and the really happy people are those who are hungry and poor and those who weep (Luke 6.20–21).

Some of Jesus's sayings about life are also paradoxes, e.g.: 'He who finds his life will lose it, and he who loses his life for my sake will find it' (Matt. 10.39).

REPETITION

There are a number of sayings in the Gospels like the paradox just quoted. The fact that they occur several times suggests that Jesus said them often. There is nothing surprising in that. Like most preachers He probably told the same stories over and over again, to different groups of people. Probably He also had favourite phrases and expressions. In Luke's Gospel we find Jesus using exactly the same words at the end of two different parables. After telling a parable about not taking the best seats at a feast Jesus said, 'Every one who exalts himself will be humbled, and he who humbles himself will be exalted' (Luke 14.11). A few chapters later we read a story about a tax-collector and a Pharisee who went to the Temple to pray, and that parable ends with the same words (Luke 18.14). Possibly the saying was added to one of the parables later on, by an editor or copyist, as a suitable conclusion. But more probably they are two different parables illustrating the same favourite saying.

THE POETIC SAYINGS OF JESUS

'We piped to you and you did not dance;
we wailed, and you did not mourn' (Matt. 11.17).

As a good teacher Jesus often put His sayings into verse. Verse is always much easier to remember than prose. Verses set to music are even easier to remember.

People remembered that when Jesus had been asked a question about John the Baptist, He had responded with a children's rhyme. He often put His own sayings into verse, although we do not always realize this, since we read a translation of what He said.

PARALLELISM IN HEBREW POETRY

One of the main characteristics of Hebrew poetry is the use of what is called 'parallelism', a sort of rhyming of ideas in which the second line of a verse is 'parallel' with the first line. We may see this by taking a brief look at some examples from the Psalms.

1. In the simplest form of parallelism the second line repeats the same idea as the first line, e.g.:

In thy strength the king rejoices, O LORD;
and in thy help how greatly he exults! (Ps. 21.1).

Both lines state that the king rejoices in the help that God has given him.

2. Sometimes the second line adds to the meaning of the first line, e.g.:

He asked life of thee; thou gavest it to him,
length of days for ever and ever (Ps. 21.4).

In this verse the second line makes it clear that God has not just given the king life, but he has given him *long* life.

3. Sometimes the two lines express the same thought in contrasting ways, e.g.:

Day to day pours forth speech,
and night to night declares knowledge (Ps. 19.2).

The children's rhyme which Jesus quoted (Matt. 11.17) expresses the same thought in opposite ways.

4. Sometimes the first line is not a complete thought, and it needs the second line to complete it, e.g.:

I cry aloud to the LORD,
and he answers me from his holy hill (Ps. 3.4).

JESUS'S POETRY

Very little of the New Testament has been set out to look like poetry, which means that we do not easily recognize it as verse. In most modern translations the Beatitudes have been arranged as poetry (Matt. 5.1–12). Much more of what Jesus said could be arranged in a similar way, e.g.:

He who is faithful in a very little
  Is faithful also in much;
and he who is dishonest in a very little
  is dishonest also in much.
If then you have not been faithful in the unrighteous mammon,
  Who will entrust to you the true riches?
And if you have not been faithful in that which is another's,
  Who will give you that which is your own?
No servant can serve two masters;
  For either he will hate the one and love the other,
  or he will be devoted to the one and despise the other.
You cannot serve God and mammon (Luke 16.10–13).

USE OF THE OLD TESTAMENT

Jesus and His disciples knew the Old Testament well. At school they had learned to read it and to recite parts of it. They heard it being read in the synagogue each sabbath. When Jesus used the Old Testament to teach His disciples, it was another example of using what was familiar. When He used Old Testament pictures and ideas the disciples felt at home, and thought they understood what He was talking about. We have already seen an example of this in His picture of the vine. In volume 2 we shall consider the subject in greater depth.

Sometimes Jesus made clear claims to fulfil Old Testament prophecies. When John the Baptist was in prison he was filled with doubts. Was Jesus after all the one for whom he had been sent to prepare the way? He sent his disciples to ask Jesus, 'Are you he who is to come, or shall we look for another?' Jesus invited them to spend some time with Him, and to see what He did. Then He sent them back to tell John what they had seen and heard. 'The blind receive their sight, the lame walk, lepers are cleansed, and the deaf hear, the dead are raised up, the poor have good news preached to them' (Luke 7.18–23). Jesus's words were echoing Isaiah's prophecy of the things that will happen when the Day of the Lord comes (Isaiah 35.5–6).

TEACHING BY EXAMPLE

The reply which Jesus sent to John shows clearly that Jesus taught by what He did as well as by what He said.

41

For example, Jesus told His disciples that they should show love and concern for the people around them, especially those people whom others despised and avoided. He taught it in parables such as the Good Samaritan. He taught it in verse. He taught it above all by His own example, in the way that He treated people. Jesus was not ashamed to be seen visiting sinners. He was kind to a prostitute and gentle with the woman caught in adultery. He went out of His way to meet Zaccheus the tax-collector. Even on the cross Jesus showed love for the robber on the next cross. (See Mark 2.15–16; Luke 7.36–50; John 8.1–11; Luke 19.1–9; 23.39.)

SYMBOLIC ACTION

Although Jesus was teaching His disciples by everything that He did and said, from time to time He deliberately did something that was even more startling than usual. He performed a symbolic action.

The Old Testament prophets had used symbolic action to show what God was going to do. For example, the prophet Ahijah tore his new robe into twelve pieces, and gave ten pieces to Jeroboam. The meaning of the action was that God was about to tear the kingdom from the hands of Solomon, and give ten tribes to Jeroboam (1 Kings 11.30–31). Jeremiah took a flask and dramatically smashed it, to show how God would break the people and the city (Jer. 19.1–19). Ezekiel packed his bags, took them outside his house, and then dug a hole through the wall of his house, as a sign that Israel would go into Exile (Ezek. 12.1–13). For the Jews, actions such as these were much more than illustrations of what might happen. A symbolic action actually helped to bring about the event which it foretold.

Jesus performed a symbolic action when He borrowed a donkey and rode it into Jerusalem. The crowd understood that He was claiming to be a king (Mark 11.1–10). When He drove the traders out of the Temple, and when He washed his disciples' feet, He was also doing things that were symbolic.

Jesus's actions at the Last Supper were full of symbolism. When He took the bread and the wine and said, 'This is my body', 'This is my blood', He was proclaiming His own death. He told His followers to continue to do it until He should return, so that it symbolizes not only His death but also His coming again. 'As often as you eat this bread and drink the cup, you proclaim the Lord's death until he comes' (1 Cor. 11.26). Christians have been meditating on the symbolism of this action ever since Jesus first performed it.

Jesus used every means at His disposal to teach His disciples, and to teach them in such a way that they would remember what He had taught. He concentrated especially on teaching the Twelve, those whom

Jesus taught all His followers, especially the Twelve, sometimes along with great crowds, sometimes on their own, using every means to ensure they would remember His words. Teachers today have books, radio, TV and other 'aids' to help them, but most Christian teaching is to gathered congregations in church or outdoors – as above in central Africa, or to children in school – as below in the Caribbean island of Bonaire.

He had chosen 'to be with him'. The Twelve were to be the foundation of the Church, and it was very important that they should remember and understand the teaching of Jesus.

There is an imaginary story about a conversation between Jesus and the angel Gabriel. After Jesus had returned to heaven Gabriel asked Him what he had done to make sure that His work on earth would be continued. Jesus replied, 'I have left twelve men.'

'Is that all?' asked Gabriel. 'Haven't you written a book?'

'No', said Jesus.

'Haven't you set up an organization?'

'No.'

'Surely you have left some written instructions?'

'No', said Jesus. 'I have just left twelve men.'

STUDY SUGGESTIONS

WORDS AND MEANINGS

1. Who is Mammon? What did Jesus mean when He said, 'You cannot serve God and Mammon'? (Luke 16.13).
2. Why are the verses found in Matt. 5.1–12 called 'The Beatitudes'?
3. What are 'parallel lines'? In which subject is the expression most commonly used?
4. Explain what is meant by the following words and phrases as used in this chapter.
   (a) 'vineyard'   (b) 'prophecies'
   (c) 'symbolic action'   (d) 'suitable conclusion'

REVIEW OF CONTENT

5. What 'teaching aids' did teachers have in the time of Jesus?
6. Explain the difference between a parable and an allegory. Give one example of each, showing why it is either a parable or an allegory.
7. Give two reasons why Jesus and His disciples knew the Old Testament well?
8. Which group of people received the most teaching from Jesus? Why was that the case, and for what purpose?

BIBLE STUDY

9. What are the particular truths that Jesus wanted to teach in each of the following parables?
   (a) The Dishonest Steward (Luke 16.1–9)
   (b) The Two Sons (Matt. 21.28–32)
   (c) The Banquet (Matt. 22.1–14)
   (d) The Fig Tree (Luke 13.6–9)
   (e) The Seed growing Secretly (Mark 4.26–29)

10. Read Mary's song in Luke 1.46–55. Select verses to exemplify:
    (a) a simple parallelism
    (b) the same idea expressed in opposite ways
    (c) the second line adding to the thought of the first line
    (d) the second line completing the sense of the first line
11. Read Isaiah 5.1–7. Which verse shows most clearly the meaning of the allegory in this passage?
12. Copy out Matthew 5.43–48, setting it out in lines as a poem.
13. Read the story of Jesus cursing the fig tree (Mark 11.12–14, 20–25). This is a difficult story to understand; what possible explanation can you find for Jesus's action?

FURTHER STUDY AND DISCUSSION

14. All of the following were 'everyday things' to Jesus and his friends. Which if any of them are *not* found in your country or culture? How does this affect your understanding of Jesus's teaching? bread (e.g. John 6.35), wine and wineskins (e.g. Mark 2.22), mill stones (e.g. Luke 17.2), thistles (e.g. Matt. 7.16), sheep and shepherds (e.g. Mark 6.34), barns (e.g. Matt. 6.26), vines and vineyards (e.g. John 15.1; Matt. 20.1), wolves (e.g. Luke 10.3), oil lamps (e.g. Matt. 25.3), fishermen (e.g. Mark 1.16), servants (e.g. Luke 17.7).
    What alternative 'everyday things' could you use to teach the same truths to different groups in your own country?
15. Discuss the use of humour and exaggeration in preaching and teaching. From your own experience suggest (a) situations in which either of them has been or could be helpful? (b) situations in which either of them has led or could lead to misunderstanding?
16. A man accused a preacher of preaching the same sermon every week. The preacher replied that he would continue to preach it until the congregation had heard it. What do you think: (a) the man meant? (b) the preacher meant?
17. Give an example of a paradox which is used in Christian doctrine. Point out what is paradoxical about it, and the reasons for using it.
18. A poor teacher is sometimes said to be 'all chalk and talk'. Think of some of the good teachers you have known. What was it that made them good teachers?
19. What methods have traditionally been used for teaching religion in your country or culture? How effective do you think they are? What are some methods of preaching and teaching which the Church can use today but were not available in the past? How much more effective are they, than the methods Jesus used?

4

The Central Events

' "I, when I am lifted up from the earth, will draw all men to myself." He said this to show by what death he was to die' (John 12.32–33).

THE CRUCIFIXION

Jesus was executed by crucifixion in Jerusalem some time at or around the Passover Festival between AD 29 and 31. This was the climax of the religious and political tensions which had centred on His life and His teaching. We shall consider why and how Jesus died.

RELIGIOUS REASONS

'This was why the Jews sought all the more to kill him, because he not only broke the sabbath, but also called God his own Father, making himself equal with God' (John 5.18). From the beginning of His ministry Jesus had come into conflict with certain of the Jewish religious leaders. It seemed to some of them that Jesus was a threat to their religious beliefs and practices. In particular, He seemed to be challenging the place of the law, which was their highest authority.

For the Pharisees the law was a combination of the Torah and the traditions that had been collected and passed down by their ancestors (see pp. 17–18). All the Gospels contain stories about Jesus breaking the law by 'working' on the sabbath, especially by healing people (e.g. Matt. 12.9–14; Mark 3.1–6; Luke 13.10–17; John 5.1–18). Apparently Jesus did not keep the Jewish tradition that holy people fasted on Mondays and Thursdays. He mixed freely with people who were 'unclean' (e.g. Gentiles, lepers, tax-collectors, prostitutes) and by doing so became ritually unclean Himself. His disciples were not strict about ritual washing. According to Mark's Gospel, Jesus was more concerned about moral purity than ritual purity (Mark 7.1–23).

A deeper cause of conflict was the way in which Jesus sometimes told people that their sins were forgiven (see e.g. Mark 2.6; Luke 7.48–49). Only God could forgive sins. Some of the Jews wondered whether this man was Himself committing the greatest sin of all, and actually claiming to be God. He certainly had a very familiar way of talking about God, and of calling God His Father (see e.g. John 5.18). Some people thought that He must receive His power from the devil himself: 'the scribes who came from Jerusalem said, "He is possessed by Beelzebul, and by the prince of demons he casts out the demons"' (Mark

3.22). Because Jesus seemed to threaten their religious beliefs they looked for ways to get rid of Him.

POLITICAL REASONS

'If we let him go on thus, everyone will believe in him, and the Romans will come and destroy both our holy place and our nation' (John 11.48). According to John's Gospel, the members of the Sanhedrin were afraid that if Jesus's ministry continued it would result in rebellion against Rome. Some of the Jews thought that Jesus was the Messiah they had been hoping for. John's Gospel tells that after the feeding of the multitude Jesus saw 'that they were about to come and take him by force and make him king', so He went quietly into the hills by Himself (John 6.15). According to Matthew the mother of James and John asked Jesus, 'Command that these two sons of mine may sit, one at your right hand and one at your left, in your kingdom' (Matt. 20.21).

The Jewish leaders knew how strong and powerful the Romans were. Any sort of political revolt would be crushed with great severity, and in the process the nation itself could easily be destroyed. Even a movement for religious reform might seem to the Romans to be a political one. The members of the Sanhedrin felt that the risks were too great. Jesus would have to die.

JESUS'S PART

In the end it was Jesus Himself who forced the issue. According to the stories which have been passed down, Jesus deliberately and openly went to Jerusalem to celebrate the Passover, knowing that the Jewish authorities wanted to kill Him. Mark's Gospel tells that 'those who followed were afraid' (Mark 10.32).

Passover was one of the major Jewish festivals, when every Jew who was able to would go to Jerusalem. There may have been as many as 100,000 pilgrims, all needing somewhere to stay, and a lamb for the Passover meal. Passover was an emotional time, for the Jews remembered how God had saved them from slavery in Egypt. To the Romans it was a tense and difficult time, when trouble might easily break out. There were always Roman soldiers stationed in Jerusalem, but at Passover time the garrison was increased. The Roman prefect in charge of Judaea moved from Caesarea, where he normally lived, and stayed in Jerusalem itself while the festival was going on.

When Jesus arrived in the city He immediately made His presence known. He rode into the city on a donkey, fulfilling a messianic prophecy in the book of Zechariah (Zech. 9.9). A crowd gathered and welcomed Him as a king, throwing coats and palm branches on to the road in front of Him. The following day, according to Matthew, Mark and Luke, Jesus caused a disturbance in the outer courtyard of the

Temple, driving out the merchants who were trading there. Jesus and His disciples stayed in Bethany, a village about one-and-a-half miles from the city, but each day He came into the city and appeared openly in the Temple. He taught His disciples there, and argued with the Jewish lawyers. On the last night of His life He did not go back to Bethany, but stayed in Jerusalem. Finally He was arrested in the middle of the night in a garden just outside the city.

THE ROMANS' PART

The Gospel writers record that it was the Jewish leaders in the first place who wanted Jesus put to death. However, it was the Romans who executed Him. We can be certain of this, because crucifixion was a Roman form of punishment. (When the Jews executed anyone, they did it by stoning them. We cannot tell whether or not the Sanhedrin had the right to condemn anyone to death in Jesus's time. The Gospels suggest that they could not, but according to Acts the Sanhedrin condemned and stoned Stephen.) Crucifixion was the Roman death penalty for slaves and for foreigners. The criminal was nailed and tied to a wooden cross, and left there to die a slow and painful death. Sometimes it took several days. In Palestine it was the punishment the Romans used for those who rebelled against their rule and those guilty of violent crime such as riot and armed robbery. Jesus also received the Roman punishment of scourging, a beating so severe that people sometimes died from it.

Clearly Jesus was not a robber, but it is easy to understand why the Romans might have seen Him as a revolutionary, and a cause of riots. They condemned Him to death, and executed Him for being a danger to the state. They executed two other criminals at the same time. Jesus died very quickly. Probably He was already weak from the beating He had been given. His disciples got permission to take His body off the cross and bury it before the sabbath began.

JESUS'S UNDERSTANDING OF THE CRUCIFIXION

Jesus did not have to die then. He could have stayed away from Jerusalem. He could have gone to another country, and carried on His ministry there. Why did He choose to go to Jerusalem at Passover, and die on a cross?

We cannot see into the mind of Jesus, to know what He thought, or how His thinking changed over the months and years. All we have is His disciples' memory of His words and deeds, which they passed on to others. All four Gospels contain accounts of Jesus's teaching about His coming death. Here is a selection of verses:

'Jesus began to show his disciples that he must go to Jerusalem and suffer many things from the elders and chief priests and scribes, and be

'Why did Jesus choose to go to Jerusalem and die on a cross? . . . He accepted that it was a part of God's plan for salvation.' On Good Friday Christians in Mexico, as in many other countries, re-enact the events of Jesus's trial and journey to Calvary, or simply walk through the streets in procession. They do it as a memorial, and a reminder that our own suffering too can be part of God's plan for our salvation.

killed' (Matt. 16.21). Almost the same words are found in Mark 8.31 and Luke 9.22.

'He began to tell them what was to happen to him, saying, "Behold, we are going up to Jerusalem; and the Son of man will be delivered to the chief priests and the scribes, and they will condemn him to death, and deliver him to the Gentiles; and they will mock him, and spit upon him, and scourge him, and kill him; and after three days he will rise"' (Mark 10.33–34).

'As the lightning flashes and lights up the sky from one side to the other, so will the Son of man be in his day. But first he must suffer many things and be rejected by this generation' (Luke 17.24–25).

'As Moses lifted up the serpent in the wilderness, so must the Son of man be lifted up, that whoever believes in him may have eternal life' (John 3.14).

From these and other verses we can see that Jesus expected to die. In Matthew 16.21 and the similar verses in Mark and Luke Jesus states simply that He would be killed. According to Mark 10.33–34 He expected to be executed by the Romans, and John 3.14 suggests death by crucifixion. Of the four passages we have quoted, three contain the word 'must'. It seems as if Jesus had come to believe that He *had* to die, perhaps even that He had to die by crucifixion. He accepted that it was a part of God's plan for salvation.

THE DISCIPLES' DISMAY

The disciples were deeply shocked by Jesus's death, in spite of His efforts to prepare them for it. They had clung on to their hope that Jesus was going to establish a kingdom in this world. Instead, His ministry had come to a sudden end. Not only was Jesus dead, but He had died by crucifixion, a way of dying that the Jews found shameful. To be 'hanged' on a cross or a gallows was seen in Jewish society as a curse from God. The disciples were left completely bewildered. According to Luke, one of them said, 'We had hoped that he was the one to redeem Israel' (Luke 24.21). Clearly those words express a past hope, one that no longer existed. The disciples were also afraid of what the Jewish authorities might do to them. John's Gospel records the doors being 'shut where the disciples were, for fear of the Jews' (John 20.19). Another story tells of Peter going fishing after the crucifixion. It sounds as if he could think of nothing else to do except to go back to the job he had before he ever met Jesus.

STUDY SUGGESTIONS

WORDS AND MEANINGS

1. Who is 'Be-elzebul'?
2. What is a 'garrison'?
3. Look up 'revolution' in a dictionary. What sort of revolution did Jesus want to bring about?

REVIEW OF CONTENT

4. (a) Give two religious reasons why the Jewish leaders wanted to kill Jesus.
   (b) Why did the Jewish leaders fear that Jesus might lead a rebellion against Rome?
5. What evidence is there that the Sanhedrin did or did not have the power to condemn people to death?
6. How did Jesus' disciples feel after He had been crucified? Why do you think they felt that way?

BIBLE STUDY

7. Each of the following passages refers to breaking the law. Say in each case what action 'broke the law' and so upset some of the Jewish leaders.
   (a) Luke 5.33 (b) Luke 7.39 (c) Luke 11.38 (d) Luke 15.2
   (e) Mark 2.23–24 (d) John 5.10
8. Which groups of people were critical of Jesus according to the following two passages?
   (a) Mark 3.6 (b) Luke 6.7
9. Read John 11.5–16. According to this story, what did the disciples fear might happen in Jerusalem?
10. How did Jesus expect to die, according to Matt. 26.2? How long before His death was Jesus speaking?
11. How does Mark 10.32–45 show that the disciples did not understand Jesus' teaching about His coming death?
12. Read the story of Jesus' trial and crucifixion in Mark 14.1–15.47, and then write an account of the events in the sort of words you would use to tell a non-Christian friend about your faith.

FURTHER STUDY AND DISCUSSION

13. The Gospels refer to several occasions when Jesus said to someone: 'Your sins are forgiven.' Why did this make some of the Jewish leaders so angry?
14. Do you think Jesus *wanted* to die? Use a concordance and a Bible, and support your arguments with references.
15. How far was it really necessary for Judas to betray Jesus? Would

Jesus not have been arrested anyway? Give reasons and references to back up your view.

16. In all four Gospels the charge brought against Jesus was that He was claiming to be King of the Jews. (Use a concordance to find the four references.) What would be likely to happen to someone who claimed, or was acclaimed by others, to be 'king' in a colonial or otherwise occupied country today?

17. Who, in your opinion, was really responsible for bringing Jesus to trial and condemning Him to death? Give reasons for your answer.

18. What would you say to someone who told you that *either* Jesus only fainted on the cross, and later revived, *or* someone else must have died in His place?

RESURRECTION AND ASCENSION

Within a few days of the crucifixion the disciples were claiming that Jesus was not dead after all. They said that God had raised Him from death, and that they had met Him.

The Bible contains several different accounts of the Resurrection of Jesus. We find descriptions of it in the four Gospels, in the Acts of the Apostles, and in 1 Corinthians. There are some differences between them as to the exact events that took place. Some writers tell of disciples finding the tomb empty. Some suggest that Jesus appeared first to the disciples in Galilee; others refer to His appearing first in Jerusalem. There are also different accounts of who was the first person to meet the risen Jesus.

The stories may seem a bit confused, but their central message is clear. The disciples had met Jesus, and knew that He was alive. It was not a ghost that they had seen: Jesus had eaten food with them, and they were able to touch Him. They had not mistaken some other person for Jesus. His body still had the marks of the nails and the spear. It was the same Jesus whom they had known before. He broke bread and gave thanks in the way that He had always done. He called them by name, and showed them the same love that He had shown during His ministry. He taught them the same things that He had taught from the beginning.

Although the disciples' experience was that Jesus was alive and real, He was alive in a new and different way. He had not merely come back to continue His earthly ministry. The disciples saw Him only occasionally over a period of a few weeks. He was able to appear among them even when they were in a locked room. He seemed to be with them and listening to them even when they could not see Him (John 20.24–27).

He was able to appear to different people in different places at more or less the same time (Luke 24.33–34).

The disciples themselves were different too. They became new people. They experienced power and authority in their lives like the power and the authority which they had seen at work in the ministry of Jesus. They explained this change in themselves by saying that Jesus had given them the Holy Spirit (see chapter 5). They believed that Jesus could do this because He was now with God in glory.

The disciples' experiences of what happened were different, but related:

1. Jesus was no longer dead, but alive. They had met Him. They called this the *Resurrection*.

2. Jesus was transformed. He now existed with God in glory. They called this the *Ascension*.

3. They experienced the power of God at work in their own lives. They called this the *Holy Spirit*.

The New Testament writers had different ways of expressing these three experiences. In Luke's account the Resurrection, the Ascension and the gift of the Holy Spirit are separate events, spread over a period of seven weeks. This was a way of emphasizing their uniqueness. According to John's Gospel the Resurrection, the Ascension and the gift of the Spirit all happened on the first Easter Day. John was emphasizing their close relationship. John shows Jesus being 'lifted up' in three phases of one continuous movement. He was lifted up on a cross, lifted up from death, and lifted up into glory. The transformation of the disciples by the Holy Spirit was the immediate result. Luke and John told the story in different ways, but both wanted to show the reality of what the disciples had experienced.

THE DISCIPLES' UNDERSTANDING

Before the disciples had these experiences, they thought of the crucifixion as the end of all their hopes. Afterwards they came to think of it as the most important event in the history of the world. They saw Jesus's death on the cross as the fulfilment of the promises which God had made to His people, as recorded in the Scriptures. Three ideas in particular from the Old Testament helped them to understand it.

1. *The suffering Servant*: They thought of Jesus as the servant whom Isaiah had prophesied would suffer:

Behold, my servant shall prosper,
he shall be exalted and lifted up,
and shall be very high . . .
He was despised and rejected by men;
a man of sorrows, and acquainted with grief; . . .

'The disciples experienced three things: Jesus was alive (the Resurrection), He was with God in glory (the Ascension), God's power was at work in their lives (the Holy Spirit).' This experience has been shared by Christians all down the ages, and expressed by poets, musicians and artists as best they can – as in the Church of the Resurrection in Johannesburg, where Easter communion is celebrated below a great mural painting of the Risen Lord.

But he was wounded for our trangressions,
  he was bruised for our iniquities;
upon him was the chastisement that made us whole,
  and with his stripes we are healed . . .
He was oppressed, and he was afflicted,
  yet he opened not his mouth; . . .
And they made his grave with the wicked
  and with a rich man in his death,
although he had done no violence,
  and there was no deceit in his mouth (Isaiah 52.13; 53.3–9).

The disciples therefore referred to Jesus as 'thy holy servant Jesus' (Acts 4.30).

2. *The Passover Lamb.* Jesus had died at Passover time. In the account of God bringing the Israelites out of Egypt, every Hebrew family killed a Passover lamb. They put the lamb's blood on the doorposts and lintel of their houses, and when the Lord came to kill the Egyptian firstborn, He 'passed over' the Hebrew homes (Exod. 12.21–27). So Paul could later write, 'Christ, our paschal (Passover) lamb, has been sacrificed' (1 Cor. 5.7).

3. *A Sacrifice for Sin.* The Jews had a complicated system of sacrifices and offerings. Technically, a sacrifice involves the killing of an animal or bird. Some of the Jewish sacrifices were intended to take away sin. In Exodus we can read a description of how Aaron and his sons were to lay their hands on a ram, kill it, and then sprinkle themselves and their clothes with its blood: 'and he and his garments shall be holy, and his sons and his sons' garments with him' (Exod. 29.9–21). So the writer of the Letter to the Hebrews would be able to say about Jesus, 'He has appeared once for all at the end of the age to put away sin by the sacrifice of himself . . . When Christ had offered for all time a single sacrifice for sins, he sat down at the right hand of God' (Heb. 9.26; 10.12).

STUDY SUGGESTIONS

WORDS AND MEANINGS

1. Explain the exact meaning of each of the following words:
   (a) 'resurrection' (b) 'ascension' (c) 'uniqueness' (d) 'transformation' (e) 'reality'.

REVIEW OF CONTENT

2. (a) What three important experiences did the disciples share soon after the death of Jesus?
   (b) What names did they give to these experiences?

3. Which three Old Testament ideas were especially helpful to the early Christians? Show how each of them helped to explain the death of Jesus.

BIBLE STUDY

4. Read Matthew 28.1–20; Mark 16.1–20; Luke 24.1–52; John 20.1–29. Note in each passage:
   (a) How many women went to the tomb?
   (b) Whom did they find there?
   (c) Who met Jesus? When and where did they meet Him?
   (d) How many times is Jesus recorded as appearing?
   (e) What were the nature of these appearances?
   Why do you think that there are differences between these four accounts?

5. Read John 21.1–23.
   (a) What details in this story make it seem like an account of Jesus's first appearance?
   (b) What details in the story show that John thought that the risen Jesus was more than 'a delusion' or even 'a spirit'?

6. Read 1 Cor. 15.3–8. According to this account written by Paul:
   (a) How many times did the risen Jesus appear?
   (b) To whom did He appear first?
   (c) To how many brethren did He appear at one time?
   (d) Does this account appear in any of the Gospels?
   (e) How many appearances does Paul mention?
   (f) What does Paul say about the empty tomb?
   (g) What indication does Paul give, as to how long a period of time was involved?

7. What did the risen Jesus teach His disciples? (See especially Luke 24.25–27, 44–49; Acts 1.3–8.) Would you agree that this was the same teaching that He gave them during His ministry? Give references to support your answer.

FURTHER STUDY AND DISCUSSION

8. After the Resurrection, where do you think Jesus was when He was not with the disciples?

9. In what ways do you think it is helpful for the Church to have three separate festivals to celebrate the Resurrection, the Ascension and the coming of the Holy Spirit? In what ways and to what extent has it been unhelpful?

10. How far do you think the Old Testament ideas that helped the disciples to understand the crucifixion of Jesus (see Q. 3 above) can also help Christians today? Which one of those ideas do you think is most helpful to Christians in your area today, and why?

11. There are many people today who say that the Resurrection never happened. They claim that the disciples only imagined that they saw the risen Jesus, or that they took away the body from the tomb and only pretended to have found the tomb empty. In the light of what has happened since the time of Jesus's death, how convincing do you find these claims?

12. If it could be *proved* one way or the other that either (a) the tomb of Jesus was *not* empty on the first Easter morning, or (b) it *was* empty, what difference, if any, would if make to your own Christian faith, and why?

13. An English bishop said that the Resurrection of Jesus was 'more than a conjuring trick with skin and bones'. What do you think he meant?

5

The Growth of the Church

BEGINNING IN JERUSALEM

'You shall be my witnesses in Jerusalem ...' (Acts 1.8).

THE GIFT OF THE SPIRIT

'You shall receive power when the Holy Spirit has come upon you' (Acts 1.8). As we saw in the last chapter, after the Resurrection and Ascension of Jesus the disciples found that they were changed people. They experienced the power of God at work in their lives. They explained this new power as the gift of the Holy Spirit.

According to Luke's account the change took place on the day of Pentecost. The Feast of Pentecost, also called the Feast of Weeks, took place seven weeks after Passover. It was a joyful festival in the middle of summer, originally held to celebrate the end of the barley harvest. Although it lasted for only one day, many Jews came to Jerusalem to join in the ceremonies in the Temple. Sacrifices and offerings were made. Two loaves made from new grain were offered to the Lord, and all the men joined in the dancing and in singing psalms. Probably Jesus's disciples went to the Temple to join in the celebrations (Acts 2.1).

Suddenly the disciples were filled with the Holy Spirit. The only way they could describe it afterwards was to speak of fire and wind. In the Old Testament fire and wind are associated with the presence of God. God was present at that moment in a new and powerful way that filled the disciples with awe and wonder, and changed their lives.

The first sign that something had happened was that they began to speak in 'other tongues'. When people 'speak in tongues' they allow themselves to make sounds which they themselves cannot understand. This was a common occurrence in the early Church. Paul described speaking in tongues as speaking 'to God' and as uttering 'mysteries in the Spirit' (1 Cor. 14.2). He said that it was the Spirit in him praying, not his mind. Those who speak in tongues let the Holy Spirit direct the sounds they make, and the words that result may not be understood by anyone present. So, Paul said, they need to pray for the power to interpret tongues (1 Cor. 14.13–16), and also to pray with their minds.

When on the Day of Pentecost the disciples of Jesus found themselves speaking in languages that were unknown to them, many of the people standing near *could* understand what they said. This was the surprising thing about it. Many Jews from distant parts of the Empire had travelled to Jerusalem for the festival. When they heard the local languages of the countries where they lived being spoken by the disciples, instead of Aramaic or Greek or Latin, they were naturally astonished, and a crowd gathered. Peter took the opportunity to preach to them.

The gift of the Spirit had changed the disciples. The same Peter who had once denied that he knew Jesus because he was afraid, now spoke out boldly. He told the crowd that the Old Testament prophecies about God pouring out His Spirit in the last days had been fulfilled. Peter said that though the authorities had crucified Jesus, God had raised Him from death. It was the risen Jesus who had given them the Spirit, and the Spirit had given them the power to speak in unknown languages.

The disciples also received power to heal people. Acts 3 describes how Peter and John healed a man who had been a cripple from birth. The man's joyful praise, singing and leaping about, drew a crowd of people to see what had happened. When Peter saw the crowd he saw another chance to preach. The whole affair caused such a disturbance that Peter and John were arrested and locked up. Next day they appeared in front of the Sanhedrin, and Peter was asked how he had done such a miracle. That was another opportunity, and Peter preached to the council. When the council ordered Peter and John not to speak in the name of Jesus they bravely answered, 'Whether it is right in the sight of God to listen to you rather than to God, you must judge; for we cannot but speak of what we have seen and heard' (Acts 4.19).

From the book of Acts we may see clearly that the gift of the Spirit had made the disciples like Jesus. Even the members of the council noticed it: 'Now when they saw the boldness of Peter and John, and perceived that they were uneducated, common men, they wondered; and they recognized that they had been with Jesus' (Acts 4.13). The disciples were now able to preach to crowds of people, as Jesus had done. Like Jesus they had the power to heal, and a lot of people came to be healed (Acts 5.12–16). Like Him they had the power to see into people's hearts (Acts 5.3).

After the crucifixion the disciples had been stunned and dismayed, and had not known what they should do. Now they knew: they had to tell everyone about Jesus. From now on they spent all their time sharing with other people what they knew about Jesus. Their work was of two main sorts:

1. They had to *preach* the good news about Jesus to those who did not yet believe in Him.

2. They had to *teach* those who believed, who had repented and been baptized.

Those two jobs, preaching and teaching, are still the work of the

Church today. The New Testament itself came to be written because of the Church's need to preach and to teach.

PREACHING

'And they went forth and preached everywhere' (Mark 16.20). To preach means to proclaim something, to announce news. Christian preaching is the public announcement of the good news about Jesus. A word which is sometimes used for preaching is 'kerygma', which comes from the Greek word for proclamation. Jesus himself proclaimed or preached the gospel. 'Jesus came into Galilee, preaching the gospel of God, and saying, "The time is fulfilled, and the kingdom of God is at hand; repent, and believe in the gospel"' (Mark 1.14–15). Paul told the Corinthian Christians that Christ had sent him to preach the gospel, and to do it in simple words. 'We preach Christ crucified' (1 Cor. 1.17, 23).

Preaching, or kerygma, is basically addressed to people *outside* the Church, to people who do not believe in Jesus nor follow Him. We read in Acts of Peter preaching to crowds of Jews, to the Jewish council, to a Roman centurion, Philip preached to Samaritans and to an Ethiopian. Paul preached to Jews and to non-Jews in many towns and cities, and he preached to rulers and kings. All preaching is done in the hope that those who listen will turn away from their former lives and begin to follow Jesus. After Paul had preached to King Agrippa: 'Agrippa said to Paul, "In a short time you think to make me a Christian!" And Paul said, "Whether short or long, I would to God that not only you but also all who hear me this day might become such as I am except for these chains"' (Acts 26.28–29). In those words Paul was expressing the nature of kerygma. Preaching means trying to proclaim the good news about Jesus Christ so that people may turn to Him in faith.

The word 'repent' really means to turn, to change direction. Following Peter's sermon on the day of Pentecost we read: 'They were cut to the heart, and said to Peter and the rest of the apostles, "Brethren, what shall we do?" And Peter said to them, "Repent, and be baptized every one of you in the name of Jesus Christ for the forgiveness of your sins; and you shall receive the gift of the Holy Spirit"' (Acts 2.37–38). These words of Peter's are very like Paul's words to King Agrippa. He was saying, 'become a follower of Christ, like me.'

If we today are to be true to the preaching of the early Church, it is important for us to study the speeches and sermons in the book of Acts. We need to remember that these were written down many years after they were preached. In most cases what we have is an outline, or a literary version, of what was actually said. (If we read aloud Peter's speech in Acts 2 it takes about three minutes. Most preachers preach for far longer than that!) Even if we do not have the whole of what

Peter and the other preachers said, we have enough to give us a fairly clear idea. The speeches in Acts have been studied very carefully by New Testament scholars, especially by C. H. Dodd. Dodd found a pattern in the speeches, and he said that the contents of the preaching contained these themes:

(a) The prophecies of the Old Testament have been fulfilled. The Messianic Age which God promised has now come with Jesus.

(b) Jesus died in fulfilment of the Scriptures, and was buried.

(c) God raised Him from death, as the Scripture foretold.

(d) Jesus has been exalted to the right hand of God.

(e) The Holy Spirit in the Church is a sign of Jesus's power and glory.

(f) Jesus will return as Judge and Saviour.

(g) Repent and be baptized.

We may notice two things in this outline of the kerygma.

1. The kerygma is based on events that had happened. Jesus had lived, He had died, He had been buried, He had risen.

2. There is a great emphasis in the speeches at the beginning of Acts on the fulfilment of Scripture. In the very early days of the Church the disciples were preaching to their fellow Jews, and for them the Old Testament was the word of God. If God had foretold in His word that Jesus would come and die, then surely every Jew should follow Him. So we read that after Paul had preached in the synagogue in Beroea the Jews 'received the word with all eagerness, examining the scriptures daily to see if these things were so' (Acts 17.11).

When people believed the preaching and repented, they were baptized. Baptism was the sign that they had turned to follow Jesus. Normally baptism meant that the new follower immediately received the gift of the Spirit, and spoke in tongues.

TEACHING

'Those who received his words were baptized, ... and they devoted themselves to the apostles' teaching and fellowship, to the breaking of bread and the prayers' (Acts 2.42). For the new disciples baptism was just a beginning. They had become part of the group of believers, and they had a great deal to learn. The apostles' second important job was to teach the new believers. Teaching is sometimes also called by its Greek name, '*didache*'.

The first converts had decided to follow Jesus, and first of all they needed to learn about Jesus. They needed to know about the most important events of His life: His suffering, His death and His resurrection. The twelve men who had been with Jesus all through His ministry now came to be known as 'apostles' (see Glossary). The apostles told all the details of Jesus's last week on earth. The terrible things that had

'The disciples had to preach about Jesus to those who did not yet believe in Him . . . when people believed the preaching, baptism was the sign that they had turned to follow Jesus' – like this girl being baptized in a river in Chota Nagpur in India.

happened to Him were still fresh in their minds, and they related the story of His death and resurrection 'with power' (Acts 4.33).

The good news, or 'gospel', which the apostles preached was the story of what God had done, and the events that they had witnessed. So they told about Pontius Pilate, about the crown of thorns and the purple robe, about Barabbas, and the soldiers gambling for Jesus's robe (see Mark 15.6–15, 24), about the women who stayed nearby and watched. They even told the things that they were ashamed of, falling asleep in the garden, denying Jesus, running away. Probably some of the new Christians were people who had seen and heard Jesus for themselves. Others had not heard any of it before, but soon they knew the details of Jesus's suffering almost as well as if they had been present.

The new followers wanted to learn as much as they could about what Jesus had said and done, and the apostles and other Christians were glad to share their knowledge. So they told of the miracles which Jesus had worked, the people He had met, the stories He had told, the things which He had taught them. In particular they remembered and told those things about Jesus which were especially useful to the new Christians. New Christians today have many questions to ask about what it means to be a Christian. The first converts in Jerusalem would surely have been just the same.

Let us imagine a group of new converts meeting with Philip and Andrew in Jerusalem:

One of the converts has noticed that some Christians share all their money, and he wants to know more. Philip tells him that when Jesus was alive they shared everything. They kept their money in a box, and Judas Iscariot looked after it. Often there was very little money. There was nowhere near enough to buy bread for 5,000 people. Because Judas looked after the money it upset him to see expensive perfume being poured on Jesus.

The new converts might also listen to Andrew speaking about a rich young ruler who came to Jesus one day. The young man asked Jesus what he should do to inherit eternal life. When Jesus told him to keep the commandments he said he already kept them. Then Jesus told him to sell everything he had and give it to the poor. He found that too hard, and went sadly way.

Perhaps another member of the group has marriage problems. He had decided to divorce his wife, when he heard one of the apostles preach, and was baptized. Now he wonders what he should do as a Chritian. He explains that he feels he married the wrong girl, and he knows exactly which girl he wants to marry now. Philip and Andrew are both certain what Jesus would have said, especially since the man's wife has not been unfaithful to him. Jesus would have said that to marry another woman was to commit adultery. Philip remembers Jesus saying that even to look at another woman and *want* to marry her was to commit adultery.

Someone else has a question about paying taxes. Perhaps he is a man who hates the Romans. Now that he is a member of the Kingdom of God he feels he need not pay any Roman taxes. Andrew tells him at once that followers of Jesus have to pay their taxes. Andrew remembers how Jesus paid His taxes. He also tells how Jesus's enemies had once tried to trick Him with a question about paying taxes. Jesus had asked them to show Him a coin. When they did so He pointed to Caesar's head on the coin, and said, 'Render to Caesar the things that are Caesar's, and to God the things that are God's' (Mark 12.17).

One of the women there wants to know how long it will be before Jesus comes back. Philip and Andrew think it will be very soon, perhaps only a matter of days or weeks. But they do not know how soon. They remember asking Jesus that question when He was alive, and He told them that even He Himself did not know when it would be.

We have just *imagined* this group of new converts meeting with Philip and Andrew. No doubt the conversation we suggested is much over-simplified. However it is the sort of thing that must have happened all the time in the very early days after the coming of the Spirit. Perhaps it was after such a conversation that a young Christian called Barnabas sold a field that he owned, and gave the money to the apostles (Acts 4.37). The Twelve shared with the new Christians all their knowledge of Jesus. Jesus had promised that when the Spirit came 'he will bring to your remembrance all that I have said to you' (John 14.26). So they were guided by the Spirit and by the questions which the converts asked. The stories about what Jesus had said and done were told over and over again, so that the details were fixed in the minds of those who told them. They were passed from believer to believer. No one had any need to write them down at that time.

THE WORK OF THE CHURCH

'Every day in the temple and at home they did not cease teaching and preaching Jesus as the Christ' (Acts 5.42). We have seen that the apostles had two related but distinct jobs to do. There was the task of *preaching*, proclaiming the good news about what God had done in Jesus, and inviting the hearers to turn and follow Him. Kerygma was always directed to non-believers. Then there was the task of *teaching*, instructing those who had been baptized and begun to follow Jesus. Teaching was always directed to Christians.

The followers of Jesus did not only preach and teach by what they said. Like Jesus Himself, they proclaimed their message in the way that they *lived*. They had to show by their lives and their actions that the kingdom of God had really come. So we read in Acts that they shared their property, cared for widows, healed the sick: 'Many wonders and signs were done through the apostles. And all who believed were together and had all things in common; and they sold their possessions and goods and distributed them to all, as any had need. And day by day, attending the temple together and breaking bread in their homes, they partook of food with glad and generous hearts, praising God and having favour with all the people. And the Lord added to their number day by day those who were being saved' (Acts 2.43–47).

STUDY SUGGESTIONS

WORDS AND MEANINGS

1. Our word 'gospel' translates a Greek word '*euangelion*', meaning 'good news', which is seldom found outside the New Testament. The words 'evangelist', 'evangelize', 'evangelical' all come from this same Greek word. What does each of them mean?
2. If the Greek word '*didache*' meant 'teaching' what does the English word 'didactic' mean?

REVIEW OF CONTENT

3. What did the Jews celebrate at the Feast of Pentecost?
4. People often think that to 'repent' means to be sorry. What does it really mean? Why can it also have a sense of being sorry?
5. What was the meaning and purpose of baptism in the early Church?
6. What two things helped the early Christians to remember what Jesus had said and done?
7. Who sold a field and gave the money from it to the apostles? Why did he do it?

BIBLE STUDY

8. Luke 2.10 and Romans 10.15 both contain words which could also be translated 'gospel'. What are those words?
9. Read Acts 2.1–4. Which of the following Old Testament passages describe the presence of God and His Spirit in the same sort of way, i.e. as 'wind' and 'fire'? What other descriptions of His presence do you find in them?
   (a) Exod. 13.21–22   (b) Deut. 5.22   (c) Ps. 18.6–14
   (d) Ps. 29.3   (e) Ps. 68.7–8   (f) Ps. 104.1–4   (g) Isa. 66.15.
10. (a) The Hebrew word '*ruach*' can mean spirit, breath, or wind. Read the Creation story in Genesis 2.4–9. Which verse describes

how God formed man and breathed His *ruach* into him, and which phrase translates *ruach* in that verse?

(b) In the New Testament the Greek word '*pneuma*' has similar meanings. Read John 3.1–10. In which verse does Jesus say 'the "*pneuma*" blows where it wills', and which English word translates *pneuma* in that verse?

11. Read Acts 17.22–31.

   (a) In what ways does Paul's speech to the Athenians differ from the speeches at the beginning of Acts, and from the outline of the kerygma given in this chapter?

   (b) How do you account for those differences?

12. What did Jesus mean when He said 'Render to Caesar the things that are Caesar's' (Mark 12.13–17)? (Some readers may find it helpful to consult a commentary before answering this question.)

FURTHER STUDY AND DISCUSSION

13. If we want people to hear the good news, in what ways is it important:

   (a) to follow the pattern of the speeches at the beginning of Acts?

   (b) to express the message in words and symbols which the hearers will understand?

14. The apostles knew that they had a two-fold ministry, to those who were not yet Christians, and to those who were already Christians. In what chief ways does your own Church carry out these two parts of its ministry? Which part does it consider most important, and why? Do you feel that either part is neglected? If so, in what ways, and what could be done to improve matters?

15. In some countries Christians are or have been forbidden to preach the gospel. How is it that the good news of Jesus has still continued to be spread in those countries?

16. Look up Jesus's teaching on divorce in Mark 10.11–12 and Matthew 19.9. Why do you think there is a difference between the accounts in these two Gospels?

18. Just as the kerygma was based on the events which had happened, so are the creeds which we recite. Why are those events of such importance to Christians?

19. Find out as much as you can about the subject of speaking in tongues. If you have ever spoken in tongues yourself, or heard others doing so, write a brief account of the experience. If you can, discuss it with others who have had similar experiences. How far does Paul's description in 1 Cor. 14 coincide with your own experience? What do you think is the value of speaking in tongues for Christians today?

SPREADING INTO THE WORLD

'... and in all Judaea and Samaria and to the end of the earth' (Acts 1.8).

A JEWISH CHURCH

'Speaking the word to none except Jews' (Acts 11.19). Jesus was a Jew. All His disciples were Jews. The Church began in Jerusalem, and in its early days all Christians were Jews. Christianity began as a group within Judaism, a sect, just as Shi'ites are a group within Islam and the Arya-Samaj a group within Hinduism. Although people had come from many countries to Jerusalem for the feast of Pentecost, and they heard the disciples speaking to them in their own languages, they were still all Jews. The things which marked a Jew as a Jew were that he had been circumcised and that he kept the law of Moses: 'At the end of eight days, when he was circumcised, he was called Jesus' (Luke 2.21).

JEWS OF THE DISPERSION

Thousands of Jews, known as the Jews of the '*diaspora*', or 'Dispersion', lived away from Palestine. This widespread settlement of Jews began six centuries before the birth of Jesus. By the 1st century BC the Greek historian, Strabo, could say that Jews were to be found in every city. (Even today the majority of Jews live away from Palestine.) In the 1st century AD the Jews of the Dispersion usually spoke Greek, while Jews who lived in Palestine spoke Aramaic. Most of them paid the half-shekel tax for the support of the Temple. Wherever they lived they kept the Jewish food laws, observed the sabbath, only married other Jews, and had their baby boys circumcised on the eighth day. In many cultures circumcision is a sign that a boy has become a man. For Jews circumcision is a sign of being a Jew, bound to keep the Law of Moses.

The Law of Moses states that at the great festivals all the men should go to Jerusalem to worship God (Deut. 16.16–17). Many of the Jews of the Dispersion lived too far away to go to Jerusalem three times a year, or even once a year, but they went when they were able to. This is the reason why the city was full of pilgrims at Passover and at Pentecost. Some Greek-speaking Jews lived in Jerusalem, and had their own synagogues, where Greek was the language used (Acts 6.9).

PROSELYTES AND GOD-FEARERS

At the time of Jesus many people were attracted by the Jewish religion. The Jews worshipped one God. They had high moral standards, believing that God wanted them to be kind to widows and orphans, to foreigners and slaves. However they also believed that they, and only they, were God's chosen people. They called all non-Jews 'Gentiles', and believed that Gentiles were unclean. For a Jew the whole world is divided into two sorts of people, Jews who keep the Law, and Gentiles who do not keep the Law.

A Gentile can become a Jew. To do that he has to agree that he will keep the Law of Moses, and be circumcised as a sign of keeping the Law. A person who becomes a Jew in this way is called a 'proselyte'.

In the time of Jesus a number of Gentiles would have liked to follow part of the Jewish religion, but they were not prepared to accept the whole of the Law and be circumcised. The Law is full of ritual instructions about washing and food and sacrifices. If someone became a proselyte he would be cut off from the rest of his family who had remained Gentiles. For these reasons there were Gentiles who liked to worship in the synagogue, who read the Old Testament, and kept the Jewish hours of prayer, but who did not take the big step of actually becoming Jews. People like this were called 'God-fearers'. The centurion who asked Jesus to heal his servant was one of these Gentiles. The elders who took his message to Jesus said, 'He loves our nation and he built us our synagogue' (Luke 7.5).

The centurion did not go to Jesus himself, or expect Jesus to enter his house. He knew that Jews did not normally enter the houses of Gentiles. For the same reason John's Gospel tells us that at the trial of Jesus the Jews would not enter the Praetorium to speak to Pontius Pilate. To enter the Praetorium would have made them unclean, so Pilate went out to them (John 18.28–29). To eat food with a Gentile would have been even worse. No Jew would ever have thought of doing such a thing.

JEWISH DIVISIONS WITHIN THE CHURCH

Although the first Christians were all Jews, they were not all the same sort of Jew. One of the early problems they had to face was the tension between the Greek-speaking disciples and the Aramaic-speaking ones. There was a dispute about the way they were sharing things with their most needy members. The Hellenists (i.e. the Greek-speaking Jews) complained that their widows were not being given as large a share as the Hebrew (i.e. Aramaic-speaking) widows. The apostles were busy preaching and teaching, and did not want to spend time sorting out a dispute of this sort. They also recognized that they themselves were all Palestinian Jews. Perhaps there really had been some prejudice in the distribution. After praying about it they appointed seven men to positions of leadership in the Church. Those seven men were all Greek-speaking, and one of them was a proselyte (Acts 6.1–6). However that did not change the fact that at that time all the Christians were Jews, and they were preaching the gospel only to their fellow Jews.

MOVING OUT FROM JERUSALEM

'On that day a great persecution arose against the church in Jerusalem; and they were all scattered throughout the region of Judaea and Samaria, except the apostles ... Now those who were scattered went about preaching the word' (Acts 8.1, 4). One of the Hellenist leaders of the Church in Jerusalem was Stephen. He roused the fury of the Jewish authorities by questioning the importance of the Temple and the Law. It may be that Stephen was the first Christian to understand that the Temple and the Law of Moses were not essential for followers of Jesus. The Sanhedrin tried Stephen and executed him (Acts 6.8–7.60). In the persecution which followed Stephen's death the Christians in Jerusalem scattered. Some went only to other places in Judaea or to Samaria. Others went 'as far as Phoenicia and Cyprus and Antioch' (Acts 11.19). Wherever they went they told others about Jesus, believing that He was the fulfilment of their Jewish faith.

The Church was spreading, but so far only among Jews.

THE FIRST GENTILE CHRISTIANS

'But there were some of them, men of Cyprus and Cyrene, who on coming to Antioch spoke to the Greeks also, preaching the Lord Jesus. And the hand of the Lord was with them, and a great number that believed turned to the Lord' (Acts 11.20–21). 'Greeks' in this verse means Gentiles. The Church in Jerusalem sent Barnabas to follow up the work in Antioch, and later he invited Paul to help him. Both Paul and Barnabas were Jews of the Dispersion, and more accustomed to dealing with Gentiles than Palestinian Jews were.

It was especially hard for Palestinian Jewish Christians to accept that the good news was for Gentiles as well as Jews. It needed a vision and the experience of meeting Cornelius to convince Peter that God wanted the Gentiles in the Church (Acts 10).

BAPTISM AND CIRCUMCISION

'Some men came down from Judaea and were teaching the brethren, "Unless you are circumcised according to the custom of Moses, you cannot be saved"' (Acts 15.1). Baptism is the sign that a person has become a follower of Jesus. Circumcision is the sign of becoming a Jew and keeping the law of Moses. When the first Gentiles were baptized and began to follow Jesus, there were Jewish Christians who thought that they should also be circumcised. Some even felt that salvation was impossible without circumcision. This situation is described in Acts, and is referred to in some of the New Testament letters.

According to Acts it was settled at a meeting in Jerusalem, where the Church leaders agreed that it was not necessary for Gentile Christians to be circumcised. The letter which Paul and Barnabas took back to

Antioch said: 'It has seemed good to the Holy Spirit and to us to lay upon you no greater burden than these necessary things; that you abstain from what has been sacrificed to idols and from blood and from what is strangled and from unchastity' (Acts 15.28–28). It appears that not all the Christians were satisfied on this point. Paul continued to have problems with Jewish Christians who told his converts that baptism was not enough. They needed to be circumcised as well. Paul wrote about circumcision at length in his letters to Rome and Galatia.

PAUL'S MISSIONARY WORK

'For I am not ashamed of the gospel: it is the power of God for salvation to every one who has faith, to the Jew first and also to the Greek' (Romans 1.16). When the Church leaders agreed that the gospel was for Gentiles as well as for Jews, the Church took a great step forward. Now they were ready to preach the gospel in all the world.

We have very little information about how they did it. According to the tradition of the Church, Thomas went to India, and Peter went to Rome. We know that Peter spent some time in Antioch and possibly went to Corinth (Gal. 2.11; 1 Cor. 1.12). We know scarcely anything about what the other apostles did, or where they went. The person we know the most about is Paul, so we shall consider how Paul set about his missionary work.

PAUL IN ANTIOCH IN PISIDIA

The writer of Acts describes how the Church in Antioch set Paul and Barnabas 'apart' for the work to which God had called them, and sent them off (Acts 13.2–3). They travelled many miles, by sea and land, preaching about Jesus wherever they went. In Acts 13.14–51 we can read of what they did in one city. (Antioch in Pisidia is a different city from Syrian Antioch where the gospel was first preached to Gentiles.)

On the sabbath Paul and Barnabas went to the synagogue (v. 14). Most cities and towns where Jews lived had a synagogue. After the usual readings from the Scriptures Paul was invited to speak. He took the opportunity to proclaim that in Jesus God had fulfilled His promise of salvation (v. 23). Paul told how Jesus had been condemned, killed, and buried, and how God had raised Him from the dead (vv. 27–30). Through Jesus forgiveness and freedom were offered to those who believed, but judgement would come to those who did not believe (vv. 38–41).

The congregation listened with interest, and asked Paul to come again the following week (v. 42). By the next sabbath the news had spread, so that a great crowd, including many Gentiles, gathered at the synagogue. Some of the Jews became aware that what Paul was preaching was a threat to Judaism and the Law of Moses. Afraid and

'When Church leaders agreed that the gospel was for Gentiles as well as Jews, they were ready to go and preach in all the world.' Though the gospel has since been preached in almost every country, still millions of people have never heard it. Different Churches go about the task of evangelism in different ways, and there are many new movements, like the 'hot-gospellers' above with their loud-speakers in Antigua, or the 'prophets' of the many Independent Churches in various parts of Africa and elsewhere.

jealous, they argued against what Paul was saying. Paul and Barnabas proclaimed that the good news was for the Gentiles as well, the more so because the Jews rejected it. Many Gentiles believed, but the Jews made trouble for Paul and Barnabas, and drove them out of the city.

A PATTERN OF EVENTS

Paul and Barnabas left Antioch in Pisidia and went on to Iconium, where the same events were repeated (Acts 14.1–6). They moved on to Lystra, where Paul was stoned (Acts 14.6, 19–20). However, the good news had been preached in those cities. People had become followers of Jesus. The Church had been 'planted'. (For places mentioned in Paul's and other New Testament letters, see map, p. 83.)

Paul's next job was to teach the new disciples, but he was prevented from doing that when he was driven out. However he and Barnabas revisited those three cities when things had quietened down: 'They returned to Lystra and to Iconium and to Antioch, strengthening the souls of the disciples, exhorting them to continue in the faith, and saying that through many tribulations we must enter the kingdom of God. And when they had appointed elders for them in every church, with prayer and fasting, they committed them to the Lord in whom they believed.' (Acts 14.21–23.)

On their second visit Paul and Barnabas were not concerned to preach the gospel to non-believers. That had become the job of the Christians who lived there. Paul's concern now was to teach. We may imagine they went quietly into the city and stayed in the home of a Christian there. They spent their time 'strengthening' and 'exhorting' the new Christians, in what we might call 'pastoral care'. Finally they appointed 'elders' to be the leaders of the new Christian community.

Paul never stayed long in one place. Later he would spend eighteen months in Corinth and three years in Ephesus, but often he stayed for only a few weeks. He was kept moving by the overwhelming need to proclaim the gospel to as many people as possible before the expected return of Jesus in glory. Whenever Paul went to a new town or city he followed the same pattern as far as possible. He went to the synagogue on the sabbath and preached to the Jews first. Some Jews believed, but often most of those who believed were Gentiles. The believers were baptized, and a new local Church had begun.

Paul was always concerned for the Churches which had been started through his preaching. We have already noticed that he revisited the converts in Antioch in Pisidia, Lystra and Iconium on his way back to Antioch. After spending some time in Antioch and Jerusalem Paul was ready to set out again. His first thought was to see how the new Christians were getting on. 'After some days Paul said to Barnabas, "Come, let us return and visit the brethren in every city where we proclaimed the word of the Lord, and see how they are" ... And he went through Syria and Cilicia, strengthening the churches. And he came also to Derbe and to Lystra ... So the churches were strengthened in the faith, and they increased in numbers daily' (Acts 15.36, 41; 16.1, 5). The help and support were mutual. Paul instructed the young Christians. They gave him hospitality, and their faith encouraged him.

We can see that Paul in his work as a missionary was concerned with both aspects of the Church's two-fold ministry. He proclaimed the gospel to those who had not heard it before, and he taught those who believed. It was the need of Christians to be taught which led to the first Christian writings which have come down to us.

STUDY SUGGESTIONS

WORDS AND MEANINGS

1. Which of the following phrases has the same meaning as 'essential':
   (a) not important?   (b) fairly important?
   (c) very important?   (d) absolutely necessary?
2. (a) What name is given to a Gentile who has become a Jew?
   (b) What do we call the Jews who live outside Palestine?
   (c) Why were Greek-speaking Jews known as 'Hellenists'?

REVIEW OF CONTENT

3. What did the God-fearers:
   (a) find attractive about Judaism?
   (b) find unattractive about Judaism?
4. Why did many God-fearers become Christians when they heard the gospel preached?
5. What made it hard for Jewish Christians to accept that the good news was for Gentiles as well as Jews?
6. Why did Paul seldom stay long in one place?
7. In what ways did the Jewish authorities think that the preaching of Stephen, and later of Paul, was a threat?

BIBLE STUDY

8. Read the story of Cornelius in Acts 10.
   (a) What details in this story show that Cornelius was a God-fearer?
   (b) What details show the usual relationship between Jews and Gentiles?
   (c) What is the significance of the phrase 'common or unclean' in this story?

(d) Why was Peter convinced that he had to baptize Cornelius and his family?

9. In Acts 11.2 and Galatians 2.12 we find the expression 'the circumcision party'. To which group of people does this phrase refer?

10. Acts 6.1–6 contains the account of the Seven being chosen by the apostles. How do we know that they were Greek-speaking Jews?

FURTHER STUDY AND DISCUSSION

11. Is Baptism considered an essential condition of membership of your Church? If not, what are the conditions of becoming a member? If Baptism is a requirement, is baptism alone enough, or are there other requirements as well? In view of the decision of the early Church regarding membership, do you think that any changes should be made in present-day Church practice?

12. 'God shows no partiality' (Acts 10.34). What divisions, if any, exist within your Church, e.g. between racial groups, tribes, castes, classes? What divisions exist between your Church and other Churches in your area? What efforts, if any, have been made to overcome these divisions? What further steps would you suggest?

13. What sort of local leaders does your Church have? Consider what is expected of your local leaders, and whether or not they are like the elders whom Paul and Barnabas appointed.

6

Writing Letters

LETTERS TO YOUNG CHURCHES

'I do not write this to make you ashamed, but to admonish you as my beloved children. For though you have countless guides in Christ, you do not have many fathers. For I became your father in Christ Jesus through the gospel' (1 Cor. 4.14–15).

When Paul preached the gospel and people believed and turned to Jesus, he became in some sense a father to the new converts, and felt a father's responsibility towards them. It was as a result of such fatherly care and concern that Paul and other leaders in the early Church wrote letters.

The part of the New Testament which is often called 'the Epistles' is a collection of the letters which they wrote ('epistle' is simply an old-fashioned English word meaning 'letter'). The New Testament letters were written by leaders of the early Church to Christian groups and individuals.

PART OF THE TEACHING MINISTRY

All the New Testament letters were written to Christians. Not one of them is addressed to a non-believer. Not one of them is written in the hope that the reader will be converted. They are a part of the teaching which the apostles and Church leaders gave to those who already believed and were baptized. Here are the opening greetings of several New Testament letters:

'To all God's beloved in Rome, who are called to be saints' (Romans 1.7).

'To the church of God which is at Corinth' (1 Cor. 1.2).

'To the saints and faithful brethren in Christ at Colossae' (Col. 1.2).

'To Philemon, our beloved fellow worker' (Philemon 1).

'To those who have obtained a faith of equal standing with ours in the righteousness of our God and Saviour Jesus Christ' (2 Peter 1.1).

We have already seen that the early Church in Jerusalem did not need books about Jesus. The apostles were there, with them, and the new Christians could ask them questions at any time. As the Church spread there was less opportunity to ask questions of the people who had known Jesus. Paul did not stay long in the towns where he preached. He appointed elders, but they were as young in the faith as the others. Paul revisited the new Christians when he had the chance, but it was not always possible. When he did not visit them he wrote them letters.

When we look at the letters of Paul which we have in the New Testament it is easy to see that they are a part of his teaching ministry. The letters which Paul wrote to the Christians in Thessalonica are a good example of teaching by letter.

LETTERS TO THE THESSALONIAN CHURCH

Thessalonica was a town in Macedonia, which Paul first visited on his second missionary journey. We can read in Acts 17 how he preached in the synagogue there, and some of those who heard believed. The unbelieving Jews were jealous and caused a disturbance, so the new Christians sent Paul and his friends to Beroea, a town nearby. In Beroea too a number of people believed, but Jews came from Thessalonica and stirred up more trouble. This time the Christians made sure that Paul went right away. Silas and Timothy stayed in Macedonia, but Paul was taken by sea as far as Athens. His Macedonian Christian friends left him there, and he sent a message back that Silas and Timothy should join him as soon as they could (Acts 17.1–15). Paul preached in Athens and then moved on to Corinth, where he stayed for eighteen months. When Silas and Timothy joined him there they found him busy preaching the gospel (Acts 18.5).

There are two letters to the Thessalonian Christians in the New Testament. Some biblical scholars doubt whether both of them were written by Paul himself. They think that a disciple of Paul either wrote or edited the second letter. However, both the letters fit in well with the story in Acts, and many people accept that Paul wrote them. They are short letters, and we shall take a brief look at them.

1 THESSALONIANS

Paul began this letter by reminding the Thessalonian Christians of his stay in their town. He said what a splendid example they had been to others in Macedonia, by the way they had turned from worshipping idols to serve the living God and wait for the return of Jesus (1 Thess. 1.7–10). Paul reminded them how he himself had been treated in Philippi (1 Thess. 2.2; cf. Acts 16.12–40), and how since then the Thessalonian Christians themselves had been persecuted (1 Thess. 2.14). He said how sad he was that he had been forced to leave Thessalonica after such a short time. He wanted to see them again, but Satan had prevented it (1 Thess. 2.17–18). Perhaps Paul had hoped to return quietly from Beroea, but his enemies had made that impossible. However, for their sakes he had been willing to go alone to Athens, and had sent Timothy to them. From this we see that Timothy had not just stayed behind in Beroea, but had been sent back to Thessalonica to

'Paul became in some sense a father to the new converts.' He revisited them when possible, and wrote letters reminding them how to live as Christians. Today Christian leaders can keep in touch with their Churches through newsletters and magazines, but they also visit local congregations, either formally, or informally like the bishop pictured here with a group of confirmation candidates in Malawi.

help the new Christians there. Timothy's job was to give them the teaching that Paul had been prevented from giving. 'We sent Timothy . . . to establish you in your faith and to exhort you' (1 Thess. 3.2).

Paul's reason for writing this letter was that Timothy had just joined him, presumably in Corinth. He had brought good news from the Thessalonian Church, and had told Paul about the faith and love that the new Christians were showing. This news had filled Paul with joy (1 Thess. 3.9).

Some of the news, however, seems to have worried Paul. He felt it necessary to remind them, 'This is the will of God . . . that each one of you know how to take a wife for himself in holiness and honour . . . that no man transgress and wrong his brother in this matter.' He also told them 'to aspire to live quietly, to mind your own affairs, and to work with your hands, as we charged you; so that you may command the respect of outsiders, and be dependent on nobody' (1 Thess. 4.3–6, 11–12).

When we look carefully at 1 Thess. 4.1, 2, 6, 11 we see that Paul was not teaching the Thessalonian Christians anything new. Paul and Timothy had already taught them, by word and example, how to live as Christians. In his letter Paul was only reminding them of that teaching. However, he had another purpose in writing besides telling them things which they already knew.

It appears from this letter that some of the Thessalonian Christians had died, and this was worrying the others. They had expected Jesus to return before anyone died. Their Christian brothers had gone to the world of the dead, a world where according to Jewish belief the living God had no place. Timothy was with them at the time, but Timothy himself was a new Christian, and may have been as puzzled as the rest of them. Silas was working in another town, so Timothy had promised to ask Paul about the matter as soon as he could.

Paul's answer is here: 'We would not have you ignorant, brethren, concerning those who are asleep, that you may not grieve as others do who have no hope. For since we believe that Jesus died and rose again, even so, through Jesus, God will bring with him those who have fallen asleep. For this we declare to you by the word of the Lord, that we who are alive, who are left until the coming of the Lord, shall not precede those who have fallen asleep. For the Lord himself will descend from heaven with a cry of command, with the archangel's call, and with the sound of the trumpet of God. And the dead in Christ will rise first; then we who are alive, who are left, shall be caught up together with them in the clouds to meet the Lord in the air; and so we shall always be with the Lord' (1 Thess. 4.13–17).

We may notice in v. 15 that Paul said it was Jesus's own teaching which he was giving. He also expected the second coming of Jesus to be soon, in his own lifetime. Paul went on to share more of Jesus's teaching about the second coming. He reminded the Thessalonians that the day of the Lord would come 'like a thief in the night' (1 Thess. 5.2; and see Matt. 24.42–44). For this reason Paul exhorted the Christians in Thessalonica to 'keep awake and be sober'.

He ended his letter with a request for prayer, a greeting to all the brethren, and instructions that his letter should be read to them (1 Thess. 5.25–27).

2 THESSALONIANS

If Paul wrote this letter also, he wrote it while Timothy and Silas were still with him: 'Paul, Silvanus and Timothy, to the church of the Thessalonians' (Silvanus was the Latin form of Silas's name). Probably this second letter was written soon after the first one. We see from 2 Thess. 2.1–2 that the Thessalonian Christians were still worrying about the return of Jesus. Paul told them 'not to be quickly shaken in mind or excited' – which tells us that they *were* 'shaken in mind and excited'. They believed that Jesus was about to return, and they were assembling to meet Him.

How could Paul have known what was happening in Thessalonica? Perhaps a Christian merchant from Macedonia was passing through Corinth and had told him. Maybe someone had written him a letter. Paul also learned that some of the Thessalonian Christians had given up their jobs: 'We hear that some of you are living in idleness, mere busybodies, not doing any work' (2 Thess. 3.11). The Christians in Thessalonica had received a letter which looked like a letter from him. It was a forgery, a 'letter purporting to be from us' (2 Thess. 2.2). Apparently it was this letter which had told them 'that the day of the Lord has come'.

This was disturbing news for Paul. Someone was writing letters in his name, and upsetting new Christians for whom he felt responsible. Paul's concern for the Christians in Thessalonica caused him to write to them a second time. He was severe with those who had given up their jobs. They should follow the example which Paul and his friends had set them: 'You yourselves know how you ought to imitate us; we were not idle when we were with you, we did not eat anyone's bread without paying, but with toil and labour we worked night and day, that we might not burden any of you. It was not because we have not that right, but to give you in our conduct an example to imitate' (2 Thess. 3.7–9).

Paul used a secretary to do the actual writing of his letters, and it was not the custom in those days to sign letters. However, Paul thought of a way to show whether or not a letter was really from him. He would write the last few sentences in his own handwriting: 'I, Paul, write this greeting with my own hand. This is the mark in every letter of mine: it is the way I write. The grace of our Lord Jesus Christ be with you all' (2 Thess. 3.17–18).

PERSONAL LETTERS

Paul told the Thessalonian Christians that he constantly remembered them in his prayers (1 Thess. 1.2; 2 Thess. 1.11). If he had been able to stay in Thessalonica he would have told them all they needed to know. Since he was not there to tell them in person he wrote them letters. Both letters are very tactful. Paul starts by praising the Thessalonian Christians for their growing faith and love, and for the way they had held to their faith in persecution and trouble. Nevertheless, we can see that they are real letters, letters which Paul wrote to friends whom he cared about. Paul never thought that he was writing a book, or that other people would be reading his letters 1900 years later. He expected that only the Christians in Thessalonica would read what he had written. He even felt it necessary to tell them to read it to all the brethren.

STUDY SUGGESTIONS

WORDS AND MEANINGS

1. Explain the meaning of 'epistle'.
2. What is the meaning of 'establish' as used in the phrase 'establish you in the faith'?

REVIEW OF CONTENT

3. What evidence is there that the New Testament letters are part of the teaching ministry of the Church?
4. What sort of relationship did Paul feel he had with those who had become Christians through his preaching?
5. What news did Timothy bring from Thessalonica when he met Paul in Corinth?
6. Which words in 1 Thess. 4.15 indicate:
   (a) that Paul was giving the teaching of Jesus?
   (b) that Paul expected to be alive when Jesus returned?
7. How do we know that Paul did not expect his letter to be widely read?

BIBLE STUDY

8. Paul reminded the Thessalonians that the Day of the Lord would come unexpectedly, 'like a thief in the night'. Use a concordance to find as many New Testament passages as you can which depict the return of Jesus in this way. What do you learn from them about:

(a) who first used the picture of a thief suddenly breaking in to describe the Second Coming?

(b) the teaching methods of Paul and other apostles in the early Church?

9. Read the account of Paul's journeys in Acts 16.11–24, and find out how he had 'been shamefully treated at Philippi' (1 Thess. 2.2).

10. Read 1 Thess. 4.1–11. Which phrases make it clear that Paul was reminding his readers of what he had already taught them?

FURTHER STUDY AND DISCUSSION

11. What do you understand by the expression, 'a father in Christ Jesus'? Do you yourself have such a father? Are *you* a 'father in Christ' to someone else? What responsibilities are involved in such a relationship?

12. 'We wanted to come to you ... but Satan hindered us' (1 Thess. 2.18). What did Paul mean by 'Satan' in that verse? Who or what do you think Satan is? What are some of the ways in which Satan works in the world today, and how can we recognize him?

13. Paul's concern was for the Christians in Thessalonica in the first century AD, not for us nearly two thousand years later. What difference does this make to the way we understand his letters? In reading the Bible, how can we distinguish the teaching which was relevant for that time only, from the teaching which we need to interpret as relevant also for us today?

FIRST-CENTURY LETTER-WRITING

Thousands of ancient letters have been discovered in Egypt, and they have shown us a great deal about the writing and sending of letters in the ancient world.

A WIFE'S LETTER TO HER HUSBAND

An Egyptian woman sent this letter to her husband in about 168 BC:

'Isias to her husband Hephaestion, greeting ... I and the child and all the family are well, and think of you always. When Horus brought your letter, in which you say you are being kept in the temple of Serapis in Memphis, I immediately thanked the gods that you are well, but I was not pleased about your not coming home ... I have brought myself and your child through such bad times and great difficulties because of the price of corn. I was looking forward to things being easier with you at home, but you have not even thought about coming home, nor remembered our need, and in this long and difficult time you have sent

81

us nothing. Horus told me that you are now released from the temple, so I am thoroughly displeased. Your mother is also annoyed, so please, for her sake and mine, return to the city if you can. You will do me a favour by taking care of yourself. Goodbye.'

Every culture has its own rules and customs about letter-writing. Isias's letter shows us the letter-writing customs of that time. She did not begin 'Dear Hephaestion', or end 'Love from Isias', as we should. The custom was to begin with the writer's name, followed by the name of the person to whom the letter was written, and a greeting. Letters usually ended with a simple word like 'farewell' or 'goodbye'.

NEW TESTAMENT LETTERS

We can see the same pattern in the New Testament letters. The Church leaders in Jerusalem wrote to their Gentile brothers: 'The brethren, both the apostles and the elders, to the brethren who are of the Gentiles in Antioch and Syria and Cilicia, greeting ... Farewell' (Acts 15.23–29).

Paul too followed the custom of the time. The first letter to the Thessalonians begins: 'Paul, Silvanus and Timothy, To the church of the Thessalonians in God our Father and the Lord Jesus Christ: Grace to you and peace' (1 Thess. 1.1). Paul always used Christian greetings instead of the standard 'Greeting' and 'Goodbye', and ended with a Christian farewell, often with the words 'Grace be with you' (1 Thess. 5.28). The farewell he wrote to the Corinthian Christians ended with the 'Grace' which we often use in our Church services today: 'The grace of the Lord Jesus Christ and the love of God and the fellowship of the Holy Spirit be with you all' (2 Cor. 13.14).

WRITING MATERIALS

Isias wrote her letter in ink on paper made from the papyrus plant which grew in Egypt. Long strips cut from the plant stems were laid side by side, with other strips laid across, and all glued together. The sheet of paper was then rolled flat and dried in the sun.

Isias's letter needed only a single sheet of paper. Longer letters needed a roll, or scroll. Sheets of paper were laid edge to edge, glued together, and rolled up. Scrolls were usually about thirty feet long and ten inches deep. Some were bigger, over 100 feet long, but these were difficult to handle. The price of a roll of papyrus was about the same as a labourer's daily wage, and a long roll of good quality could cost five or six days' pay. Poorer people often sent their messages written on a piece of broken pottery.

Isias's ink was made from soot and gum, and probably her pen was made from a reed. Usually people wrote only on one side of papyrus. When writing on a roll they wrote in columns.

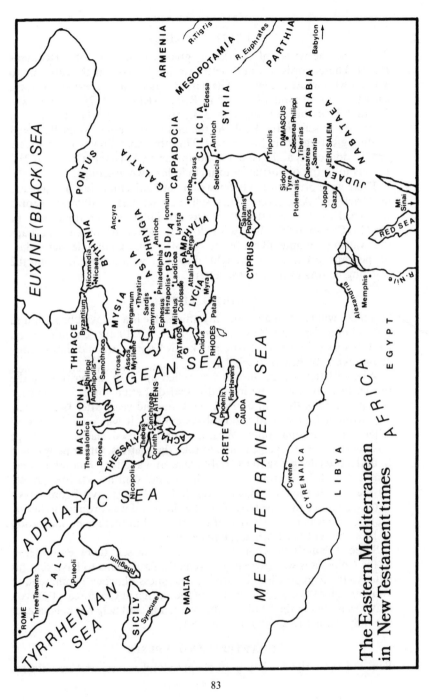

The Eastern Mediterranean in New Testament times

LETTER SCRIBES

'I Tertius, the writer of this letter, greet you in the Lord' (Romans 16.22). These words in Paul's letter to the Romans might cause us to wonder who wrote the letter. The letter begins, 'Paul, a servant of Jesus Christ . . . to all God's beloved in Rome' (Rom. 1.1, 7). So who was Tertius? Probably Tertius was a Christian friend who acted as a secretary, or scribe, for Paul. At the end of the letter, when Paul was sending greetings from his friends: 'Timothy, my fellow worker, greets you; so do Lucius and Jason and Sosipater my kinsmen' (Rom. 16.21), Tertius took the opportunity to include his own greetings.

There were professional letter-writers in Paul's time, just as there are in Africa and Asia today. They sell their services to illiterate people who need to write a letter. Paul was not illiterate, but apparently he used his Christian friends to write down the letters he dictated. Perhaps this was to save time, like a businessman or busy Church leader today, or perhaps because he thought they too would benefit from the teaching he was putting in the letters.

SENDING LETTERS

'Tychicus will tell you all about my affairs. He is a beloved brother and faithful minister and fellow servant in the Lord. I have sent him to you for this very purpose, that you may know how we are and that he may encourage your hearts' (Col. 4.7–8).

When a letter was finished it was rolled up, with the writing on the inside, tied up, and sometimes also sealed. Letter-boxes and postage stamps were not thought of until two thousand years after Isias wrote. The Roman Empire had a postal system, but it was only for official letters, not personal ones. Wealthy families used slaves, and large business firms employed carriers to take their letters. Other people had to find a traveller going to the right place, and a letter could take a long time to reach its destination. (In the second century AD one private business letter took 107 days to reach Tyre from Italy!) From Isias's letter we can see that the letter from her husband was brought to her by Horus, who was probably one of his friends, but there is no indication of how she sent her letter to Hephaestion.

Some of Paul's letters contain hints of how he sent them. Paul's letter to the Colossians was carried by Tychicus. Paul seems to have sent his letter to the Roman Church with the deaconess Phoebe: 'I commend to you our sister Phoebe, a deaconess of the church at Cenchreae, that you may receive her in the Lord as befits the saints, and help her in whatever she may require from you' (Rom. 16.1–2).

CHAPTERS AND VERSES

Paul did not write his letters in chapters and verses, and nor did his secretary. The books of the Bible were divided into the chapters that we know at the beginning of the 13th century AD, by an Englishman working at the University of Paris. In the middle of the 16th century the chapters were divided into verses.

Originally the letters, and the other books of the Bible, were simply written in paragraphs, with very little punctuation. The Readers' Digest has produced *The Readers' Bible* in which the books look much more as they first did. The writer simply moves from subject to subject. However it is very difficult to look up a particular passage in *The Readers' Bible*. The division of the biblical books into chapters and verses has made it easy to find any passage, no matter what language, translation or edition we are using.

STUDY SUGGESTIONS

WORDS AND MEANINGS

1. Explain the meaning of 'destination', 'indication'.
2. All Paul's New Testament letters end with a mention of 'grace'. What did he mean by 'grace'?

REVIEW OF CONTENT

3. Read again Isias's letter (pp. 81–82), and then say:
   (a) Where was Hephaestion, and what had he been doing?
   (b) What else had Isias received from Horus besides the letter from her husband?
   (c) What more do we learn from this letter about Hephaestion's family, and about economic conditions at the time?
4. In which country did the papyrus reed grow?
5. Why did poor people use pieces of broken pottery for sending messages?
6. In which century were the books of the Bible:
   (a) divided into chapters?   (b) divided into verses?
   Why are these divisions useful to us?

BIBLE STUDY

7. Read Philippians 2.25–29; 4.18.
   (a) Who was going to carry this letter for Paul?
   (b) Where he had come from, and for what reason?
   (c) What had recently happened to him?
8. Read the final verses of Paul's letter to the Ephesians. Who was apparently going to carry the letter to Ephesus?
9. Read 1 Cor. 16.21; Gal. 6.11; Col. 4.18. What evidence is there in

these verses to suggest that Paul used a scribe to write these letters for him?

10. Letters are often sent from more than one person. Which people joined Paul in sending:
    (a) 1 Corinthians?   (b) Philemon?
11. Tychicus was to carry Paul's letter to Colossae, but he was not going to travel on his own. Who was going with him?

FURTHER STUDY AND DISCUSSION

12. Some Christians today begin their letters 'Dear Brother –' or 'Dear Sister –', and end with 'Yours in Christ' or 'Yours in the Lord'. What do you think of this custom? Do you think that Christians should always use special greetings and farewells?
13. What forms of written Christian teaching are used today? What are the advantages of the written (or printed) word over the spoken word, for Christian teaching?
14. As we can tell from some of Paul's letters, there must have been letters written *to* him as well as those written *by* him. How much does it matter that we only have one part of the correspondence?

TREASURED LETTERS

VISITS PREFERRED

'I had much to write to you, but I would rather not write with pen and ink; I hope to see you soon, and we will talk together face to face' (3 John 13–14). These words of 'the Elder' to his friend Gaius could just as easily have been written in most of the other New Testament letters. Many of the writers say that they plan to visit the readers soon. Letters were usually a second best, written when it was not possible to 'talk together face to face'.

A LETTER PREFERRED

'I made up my mind not to make you another painful visit ... And I wrote as I did, so that when I came I might not be pained ... For I wrote you out of much affliction and anguish of heart and with many tears, not to cause you pain but to let you know the abundant love that I have for you' (2 Cor. 2.1–4). Paul decided on one occasion at least that a letter would be better than a visit. It appears, however, that he was only postponing his visit. It was *'another painful'* visit that he wanted to spare the Corinthians. In 2 Corinthians 13.1 he states that he is about to visit them for the third time.

JUST LETTERS

Clearly none of the New Testament writers thought their letters would become 'Scripture' and continue to be read for hundreds of years. (We shall consider in Volume 2 the process by which they came to be considered as Scripture.) Paul, John and the others were writing to meet immediate needs, because of news they had heard, to answer messages received, or just because someone was travelling in the right direction. Some of their letters were not even meant for sharing. For example, Paul can hardly have intended his angry words to the Galatians to be passed on: 'I wish those who unsettle you would mutilate themselves!' (Gal. 5.12).

Paul and the other letter writers did not realize how greatly their letters would be valued by those who received them. The Christians would have preferred the Church leaders' presence with them, but often that was not possible. Sometimes they were in prison. Much of the time they were busy proclaiming the gospel in new areas. In the absence of Paul and the others their letters became treasured possessions.

READ DURING WORSHIP

'I adjure you by the Lord that this letter be read to all the brethren' (1 Thess. 5.27). Paul probably expected that his letter would be read when the Christians assembled for worship. In fact, his letters were read not once, but many times. In one of his New Testament letters he gives instructions for letters to be shared with another Church: 'And when this letter has been read among you, have it read also in the church of the Laodiceans: and see that you read also the letter from Laodicea' (Col. 4.16).

COPIES

The Christians in nearby cities would soon get to know when a Church had received a letter from Paul or from another Church leader. When the Church in Thessalonica or Corinth received a letter, other Churches would ask to borrow it. They made copies, perhaps several copies. Gradually a letter that had been written to one Church about its own particular problems came to be owned and read by a number of Churches. In this way the twenty-one letters of the New Testament were preserved.

LOST LETTERS

Other letters did not survive. Paul told the Colossian Christians to read his letter to Laodicea. We do not know what happened to the letter to Laodicea, but it no longer exists. It must have been lost or destroyed at a very early date, before anyone had a chance to copy it out. We also know that Paul had written a letter to the Church in Corinth *before* he wrote the one which we call 1 Corinthians: 'I wrote to you in my letter not to associate with immoral men' (1 Cor. 5.9). Where is that letter? Some people think that a fragment of it survives in 2 Cor. 6.14—7.1, but it is equally possible that it no longer exists. What is certain is that Paul wrote a number of letters to the Christians in Corinth: 'I would not seem to be frightening you with letters. For they say, "His letters are weighty and strong, but his bodily presence is weak, and his speech of no account." Let such people understand that what we say by letter when absent, we do when present' (2 Cor. 10.9–11).

For various reasons many of Paul's letters may have been destroyed. It may be that James, Peter, John and others also wrote many letters that no longer exist. The letters which we have in the New Testament are the ones that survived, and probably just a fraction of those written by early Christian leaders.

EDITIONS

The letters that we have in the New Testament may not be exactly as they were first written. In the process of being preserved they may have been changed, sometimes by the original author, sometimes by an editor or copyist or in some cases by both.

For example, a letter that was originally written to a particular group of Christians might have been slightly altered in order to make it suitable for more general use by other Churches. This may have been done to the letters to the Ephesians and the Romans. Some people believe that 1 Peter was originally a sermon written for a service of baptism, and later altered and turned into a letter.

When the basic material in a letter was being used again, the author himself or a scribe copying it may have added passages, or altered sections. Mistakes may have been put right, and passages may have been added. When letters were copied out, parts of different letters may have been copied on to the same roll, so that what now seems to be one letter may have once been several different letters.

The technical name which is given to a new edition made in such a way is 'redaction'. We cannot be certain how many redactions of the letters there were before they reached the form in which we now have them. However the suggestion that such things happened should not surprise us when we remember the following facts:

(a) In the first century AD no one considered that the New Testament letters were 'Scripture'. People felt free to copy them and use them in whatever way seemed best.

(b) The modern idea of 'copyright' did not exist in the ancient world.

(c) Christian leaders today (and other leaders too) often use their material several times, and alter it to suit each new occasion.

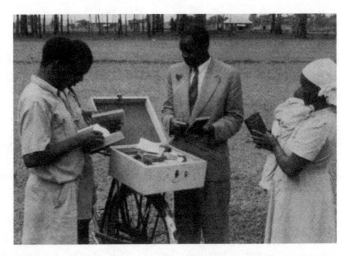

None of the New Testament writers thought their letters would become 'Scripture', though Paul did say some of his letters should be shared. But copies were passed on to other Churches, and eventually were collected and became part of the Bible. Now they are obtainable all over the world through bookshops or colporteurs – as above in East Africa, or distributed by individual Christians like the Chinese youth group in Taiwan, below, to passers-by in the street.

STUDY SUGGESTIONS

WORDS AND MEANINGS

1. What is the difference between an event which is 'postponed' and an event which is 'cancelled'?
2. What is a 'redaction'?

REVIEW OF CONTENT

3. 'Letters were a second best.' What was usually 'best'?
4. Which two Churches did Paul say were to share their letter from him?
5. Explain how it came about that some of the letters written by early Church leaders survived.
6. Which letter do we know was lost?
7. (a) Which people may have altered the original letters?
   (b) For what reasons may they have altered them?

BIBLE STUDY

8. Use a concordance to find as many references as you can in the New Testament letters where the writer states that he hopes to visit soon.

FURTHER STUDY AND DISCUSSION

9. How important do you feel it is for Church leaders to *visit* the members of their Churches?
   Is it equally important for a national Church leader, such as a bishop or a moderator, as it is for a local pastor or village catechist? If so, which people would you expect each of them to visit?
10. Consider the advantages and the disadvantages of writing down what you have to say to someone.
    Give some examples of situations where you feel a letter would be better, and of situations where a visit would be better.
11. In what circumstances, if ever, do you use again a sermon or an essay you have written for a previous occasion? Give some examples. How far did you have to alter the material, and was its impact the same on the later occasions?
12. How often, in preaching or teaching, do you use something which someone else has written? How free do you feel to make changes in it? How important do you feel it is to acknowledge when you are using someone else's words and ideas?

Special Note B: Cross-References

There is a cross-reference system in the RSV and in many other translations and editions of the Bible. This can be very useful when we are finding our way around the Bible.

For example, many of the cross-references in the New Testament tell us where Old Testament quotations can be found. In Acts we find the story of the Ethiopian eunuch:

'Now the passage of scripture which he was reading was this:

"As a sheep led to the slaughter
or a lamb before its shearers is dumb,
so he opens not his mouth ..." ' (Acts 8.32).

In the footnotes at the very bottom of the page in the RSV we see: '**8.32–33:** Isa. 53.7–8'. This tells us where in the Old Testament we can find the passage which the eunuch was reading.

The writers of the New Testament used the same ideas more than once. The cross-reference system can help us find them. Paul wrote to the Corinthians: 'Now you are the body of Christ and individually members of it' (1 Cor. 12.27). At the bottom of the page we find '**12.27:** Eph. 1.23; 4.12; Col. 1.18,24; Eph. 5.30; Rom. 12.5.' If we look up these references we discover that each one contains a reference to the Church as the body of Christ.

Many of the stories about Jesus are to be found in more than one Gospel. For example, the story of Jesus feeding five thousand people comes in all four Gospels. If we can find it in one Gospel, then by using the cross-reference system we shall be able to find it in the other three.

STUDY SUGGESTIONS

WORDS AND MEANINGS

1. What is meant by a 'cross' reference?

REVIEW OF CONTENT

2. Which of the following can you find by using the cross-reference system in the RSV:
   (a) a quotation from the Old Testament?
   (b) a similar verse or passage anywhere in the Bible?
   (c) a quotation from the Qur'an?
   (d) a quotation from any book that is not in the Bible?

(e) the same idea somewhere else in the Bible?

BIBLE STUDY

3. Find the story of the rich young ruler in Matthew 19.16–22. Find where the same story may be found in Mark and Luke.
4. 1 Peter 3.10–12 is a quotation from the Psalms. Where in the Psalms can you find it?
5. The story of the transfiguration of Jesus comes in Matthew, Mark and Luke (e.g. Mark 9.2–9). Which New Testament letter also contains a reference to the story?

FURTHER STUDY AND DISCUSSION

6. In which other translations and editions of the Bible can you find a cross-reference system? In which edition have you found the most cross-references?
7. How useful do you think a cross-reference system is? In what sort of situations would you want to use it?

7

The New Testament Letters

A man going on a long bus journey and looking out of the window may see many places of interest as the bus drives past. He can glimpse what the different landmarks look like, and where they are in relation to each other, but has no time to notice any detail. If the bus stops near one of these places, perhaps he can look at it more carefully, but still only in a limited way. If he wants to know about the country in detail he must leave the bus, and travel on foot to study each place of interest more thoroughly.

This book is rather like such a journey. We can take only a brief look at the different aspects of New Testament study, and see how they stand in relation to each other. Here and there we take a slightly closer look, like the traveller at a bus stop. One stop on our journey was at Thessalonica. The next will be Corinth. After that we shall only have a glimpse of the other letters, because we still have a long journey ahead.

DIFFERENT SORTS OF LETTERS

Anyone who writes or receives letters knows that there are different sorts of letters. Children in school learn the difference between formal and informal letters. A letter to a close friend is different from a letter to someone we have never met. A bishop writes one sort of letter to his clergy and another sort to a fellow bishop. The style of a letter varies according to the subject: for example, whether it is a matter for rejoicing or for grief, whether the letter is meant to encourage or to rebuke.

If one person can write different sorts of letters, then a collection of letters by different people will have even more variety. It is not surprising that the letters in the New Testament are very different from each other. Of the twenty-one letters, thirteen contain statements to say they were written by Paul. The remaining eight were written by other leaders in the early Church. Paul's letters are grouped together at the beginning of the collection, arranged roughly in order of length. The other eight are arranged in a similar way.

PAUL'S CORRESPONDENCE WITH CORINTH

CORINTH

Corinth was the capital of the Roman province of Achaia. Its geographical position made it a centre for trade and commerce, and in Paul's time it was the fourth most important city in the Roman Empire. People had gone from all parts of the Mediterranean world to live there, so that it had become a place of many cultures, customs and religions. The city was known for its low moral standards. Around the Empire anyone who led an immoral life was described as 'living like a Corinthian'.

PAUL'S RELATIONSHIP WITH THE CORINTHIAN CHURCH

Paul visited Corinth on his second journey. He lodged with a Jewish couple, and stayed there for eighteen months. It appears that Paul founded the Church in Corinth, for he called himself their 'father' (see p. 75). From his correspondence with Corinth we can tell that his relationship with the Christians there was often difficult. We have already seen his reference to a 'painful' visit, and the fact that he wrote them several letters. 1 Corinthians is one of the most personal and revealing letters in the New Testament. It tells us a great deal about Paul, and even more about the Corinthian Church to which he was writing.

1 CORINTHIANS

News from Corinth

It appears that Paul wrote this letter from Ephesus. Three men from the Corinthian Church had visited him there (1 Cor. 16.17). He had received a letter from Corinth (1 Cor. 7.1), so it may be that they had brought it. They had told him what was happening in the Corinthian Church.

News had also reached Paul in another way: 'It has been reported to me by Chloe's people ...' (1 Cor. 1.11). We do not know who Chloe was but she must have been someone whom Paul and the Christians in Corinth knew. Members of her household, either slaves or relatives, had brought Paul news which disturbed him greatly. The Corinthian Christians were quarrelling with each other. Different groups were claiming the authority of different Church leaders for the different things they believed and practised.

From reading 1 Corinthians we get the impression that it was the news brought by Chloe's people which drove Paul to sit down and write to Corinth, although he already had the intention of writing.

Divisions within the Church

From its beginnings the Church has always had to deal with conflict. Many of Paul's letters exhort his readers to work together in unity and love. The disunity of the Church in Corinth must have been acute to have caused him so much amazement and distress. It seems that some

Christians there were boasting that they were 'wise', and they were challenging Paul's authority: 'When I came to you, brethren, I did not come proclaiming to you the testimony of God in lofty words or wisdom. For I decided to know nothing among you except Jesus Christ and him crucified ... and my speech and my message were not in plausible words of wisdom, but in demonstration of the Spirit and of power, that your faith might not rest in the wisdom of men but in the power of God' (1 Cor. 2.1–5).

All through 1 Corinthians Paul emphasizes the need for unity. The unity of the Church is founded upon the unity of Christ: 'Is Christ divided?' (1 Cor. 1.13). Paul uses two pictures to illustrate the unity between Jesus and the Church: (a) a building, whose foundation is Jesus Christ (1 Cor. 3.10–11), and (b) a body, whose head is Christ (1 Cor. 12.12–27). Although there are varieties of gifts within the Church, 'all these are inspired by one and the same Spirit' (1 Cor. 12.11).

The marvellous passage about love in 1 Corinthians 13 is Paul's inspired response to the lack of love that the Christians in Corinth were showing. We conclude from what Paul writes elsewhere in this letter that they were being 'jealous and boastful', 'arrogant and rude', 'insisting on their own way', 'irritable and resentful'. Paul tells them: 'And I will show you a more excellent way', and praises the virtues of love, the greatest of the gifts of the Spirit.

The Causes of Division

The Corinthian Church does not seem to have been divided between Jews and Gentiles, the cause of conflict which divided so many Churches in Paul's time. We may deduce that the Christians there were mainly Gentiles, and that many of their problems were caused by the sort of city which Corinth was.

The people of Corinth were always ready to engage in lawsuits, and some Christians were accusing each other in court, instead of settling disputes amongst themselves. Reflecting the city's low standards of morality, one of the Church members was actually having sexual intercourse ('living with') his father's wife, a situation which Paul said was shocking even to pagans. In Corinth's many pagan temples meat was offered daily to idols, and the Christians were divided about whether or not they were permitted to eat meat which had been killed as a pagan sacrifice.

Some citizens of Corinth were very wealthy, while others were very poor, and the Christians had allowed this division to spoil their communion service (*agape*). Paul accused them of eating the bread and drinking the cup of the Lord 'in an unworthy manner' and 'without discerning the body' (1 Cor. 11.27–29).

Common Problems and Particular Problems

Some of the problems which faced the Corinthian Christians were problems which all Christian communities have to deal with at one time or another. Division within the Church is one such problem. There were also questions about leadership and the gifts of the Spirit, about whether or not the dead are raised, and about Christian marriage.

Other questions which divided the Corinthian Church are no longer a problem for many Churches today. For example, Christians in the West do not have to worry about eating meat which has been offered to idols. And the question about women covering their hair was special to Paul's time, when it was considered immoral for a woman to let any man except her husband see her hair. Yet arising from these particular problems Paul laid down principles that are helpful to Christians in all circumstances: e.g. 'Let no one seek his own good, but the good of his neighbour' (1 Cor. 10.24).

Paul was concerned about the conduct of worship services in Corinth; clearly the worship there was noisy and disorderly, so he laid down some rules for them (1 Cor. 14.26–33). Over the centuries, long-established Churches have developed their own rules for worship, and especially for the Eucharist or Communion service. Not all are agreed as to whether Paul's instructions on these matters are useful for us today.

Besides writing about the problems in the Church, Paul was also organizing a collection for the Christians in Jerusalem, who had been suffering from a famine. Paul's concern for them, his instructions about regular giving, and his arrangements that the money be dealt with properly are all still relevant to the Church today.

The Words of Jesus and the Words of Paul

When Paul answered the Corinthian Christians' questions about marriage, he distinguished between teaching which he knew Jesus had given, and his own opinion:

'To the married I give charge, *not I but the Lord*, that the wife should not separate from her husband and that the husband should not divorce his wife' (1 Cor. 7.10–11, and see pp. 63–64).

'To the rest *I say, not the Lord*, that if any brother has a wife who is an unbeliever and she consents to live with him, he should not divorce her' (1 Cor. 7.12).

'Now concerning the unmarried, *I have no command of the Lord*, but I give my opinion as one who by the Lord's mercy is trustworthy' (1 Cor. 7.25).

'Disunity among the Christians in Corinth must have been acute to cause Paul such distress.' The Church has always had to deal with conflict, and today perhaps even more than in Paul's time we see the devastating results of its dividedness. In Northern Ireland, for example, when the long-running 'war' between Protestants and Catholics erupted from words into violence and murder it caused untold suffering. The coffin in the bottom picture was that of a four-year-old girl killed by a sniper's bullet.

2 CORINTHIANS

The New Testament contains two letters from Paul to the Church at Corinth, but some biblical scholars think he may have written as many as five. The letter which we call 2 Corinthians may be the collected fragments of two or even three letters. Chapters 1—9 are full of Paul's relief at the good news which Titus has brought from Corinth (2 Cor. 7.6–16). A letter from Paul has grieved them, 'though only for a while ... I rejoice ... because you were grieved into repenting' (2 Cor. 7.8–9). In 2 Cor. 10.1 the tone of the letter changes, and in chapters 10—13 Paul is defending his ministry as an apostle against those who were attacking his teaching. Many scholars think this may be a part of the 'severe' letter to which Paul referred in 2 Cor. 7.

Chapters 8 and 9 concern the collection which Paul was organizing among the Macedonian Churches, and which he was now entrusting to Titus.

STUDY SUGGESTIONS

WORDS AND MEANINGS

1. Explain the meaning of the following words as used in this chapter:
   (a) 'relevant'   (b) 'distinguish'   (c) 'glimpse'   (d) 'acute'
   (e) 'plausible'
2. What do you understand by a 'long-established Church'?

REVIEW OF CONTENT

3. For what reasons are Paul's New Testament letters arranged with Romans first and Philemon last?
4. What was the importance of Corinth in the Roman Empire?
5. How many of his visits to Corinth does Paul himself refer to?
6. What quality were some of the Corinthian Christians boasting that they had?
7. Paul was organizing a charitable collection. Who was the collection for, and why did they need it?

BIBLE STUDY

8. From Acts 18.1–28 find out:
   (a) What were the names of the couple with whom Paul stayed in Corinth?
   (b) What was their trade?
   (c) Where did they go when Paul left Corinth?
   (d) Who was Apollos?
   (e) Who encouraged Apollos to go to Corinth, and what did he do there?

9. Read 1 Cor. 1.12. What were the names of the leaders of whom different groups in the Corinthian Church claimed to be followers? By what other name do we also know Cephas?

10. Read 1 Corinthians 16, and say:
    (a) Which verse suggests that Paul was writing from Ephesus?
    (b) What were the names of the three men from the Corinthian Church who visited Paul in Ephesus?
    (c) Which of Paul's friends were going to visit Corinth?
    (d) Which person did Paul want to send on a visit to Corinth, only he was not willing to go at that time?

11. Read 2 Cor. 6.14—7.1. Why do some people suggest that this is a fragment of the letter which Paul mentioned in 1 Cor. 5.9?

FURTHER STUDY AND DISCUSSION

12. How can we reconcile these two statements in 1 Corinthians: 'Any woman who prays or prophesies with her head unveiled dishonours her head' (1 Cor. 11.5) and 'the women should keep silence in the churches'? (1 Cor. 14.34)? How far do you think Christians should conform to the traditional social customs of their country?

13. Relations between Church leaders and their congregations are often difficult. If you have experienced any such difficult relations, how would you account for the difficulties? How do you think they could be overcome?

14. Consider carefully what Paul says in 1 Corinthians about the unity of the Church. In what ways can Paul's teaching help us to deal with the divisions that face us today?

15. In a certain African country the new house which the bishop urgently needed stood unfinished for several years. Because of Paul's teaching in 1 Cor. 6.1-8 the bishop refused to take the contractor to court. Do you think he was right? Give your reasons.

16. In many West African countries all the meat on sale is 'Muslim' or 'hallal' meat, and all the butchers are Muslims. They slit the animals' throats to allow the blood to run out, and as they do so they say 'Allah Akbar', 'God is great'.
    What do you think a Christian's attitude should be to eating this hallal meat?

17. The administration of money in the Church is often a cause of conflict. How did Paul make sure that no one would accuse him of using the collection for himself or for other purposes? (see 1 Cor. 16.3-4 and 2 Cor. 8.16-22).
    What does this teach those who are put in charge of Church money?

18. How far do you think Paul's instructions about the Communion

service (1 Cor. 11.17–34) and about the conduct of worship (1 Cor. 14.26–36) are of value for the Church today? To what extent are they followed in the Church you belong to?

PAUL'S OTHER NEW TESTAMENT LETTERS

As our journey continues we look more briefly at the rest of Paul's letters. They range from a short personal note to a friend to a long theological statement to a Church he had not yet visited. We discuss them here under four main headings.

1 A PERSONAL LETTER TO AN INDIVIDUAL

Philemon

Paul's letter to Philemon is so short that it was not divided into chapters; it has only twenty-five verses. Philemon was probably a member of the Church at Colossae. Paul knew him, and had probably been responsible for Philemon's becoming a Christian. Philemon's slave Onesimus had run away and met Paul, and had become a Christian (Philemon 10). Paul sent him back to his master with this letter, in which he appealed to Philemon to welcome Onesimus back, not just as a forgiven slave but as a Christian brother.

2 PERSONAL LETTERS ABOUT CHURCH ORGANIZATION

1 Timothy, 2 Timothy and Titus are often called the 'Pastoral Epistles' (from the Latin *'pastor'*, a shepherd). Timothy and Titus were both companions of Paul.

1 Timothy

1 Timothy warns against false teaching in the Church (this is discussed in volume 2). It also contains instructions about Church administration, describing the sort of people who should be appointed to be leaders in the Church: bishops (who were probably the same as elders), deacons and widows. There are instructions about women's place in the Church, and also about slaves. This letter contains almost no personal details, except that it is addressed to a young man who is advised that he should take a little wine for his stomach (1 Tim. 5.1, 23).

2 Timothy

2 Timothy is full of advice to a young colleague. There are many personal details. Timothy is asked to bring Mark, and to collect some belongings that had been left at Troas (2 Tim. 4.11–13). This letter not only warns against false teaching, but names some of the false teachers:

'Among them are Hymenaeus and Philetus, who have swerved from the truth by holding that the resurrection is past already. They are upsetting the faith of some.' (2 Tim. 2.17).

In this letter Paul is shown as awaiting execution. Many of his friends have left him, but he is still confident in the power of Christ (2 Tim. 1.15–16; 4.6, 16, 18).

Titus

The letter to Titus, like 1 Timothy, is concerned with the sort of character that Church leaders should possess: 'For a bishop, as God's steward, must be blameless' (Titus 1.7). The letter contains advice to Titus on how to teach the different groups within the Church, and also general advice about Christian conduct. It ends with very practical instructions: 'When I send Artemas or Tychicus to you, do your best to come to me in Nicopolis, because I have decided to spend the winter there' (Titus 3.12).

There are widely differing views about the origins of the Pastoral Letters. Some scholars believe they were written by Paul to his young assistants when he had left them in charge of Churches for a time. Others believe that Paul himself did *not* write these letters. They think they were written long after Paul was dead, by a writer who used Paul's name, and perhaps included fragments of letters which Paul really had written (see also note on Colossians and Ephesians, p. 102).

3 VERY PERSONAL LETTERS TO PARTICULAR CHURCHES

Some of Paul's letters were written to Churches which he knew very well, and he wrote to them about the particular problems which they were facing. We have already noticed this in his letters to the Thessalonians and the Corinthians. Paul's letters to the Philippians and to the Churches of Galatia were also very personal letters.

Galatians

No one is certain exactly who or where 'the Churches of Galatia' were. Strictly speaking the Galatians were a group of people who lived in the central part of Asia Minor. Under the Romans Galatia was the name of a large province, which included the towns of Antioch, Iconium, Lystra and Derbe, where Paul preached on his first missionary journey. It may have been the people of those cities to whom he was writing, or it could have been to Galatians living further to the north.

Whoever Paul was writing to, his reasons for writing are clear. His own Christian teaching had been attacked by Jewish Christians who said that all Christians must be circumcised and keep the Jewish law. It appears that they were saying that Paul was not an apostle, and that he was teaching a false gospel. Paul vigorously defended the gospel he had preached: 'I would have you know, brethren, that the gospel which was preached by me is not man's gospel ... it came through a revelation of Jesus Christ' (Gal. 1.11–12). Paul insisted that God Himself had made him an apostle, and that the apostles in Jerusalem had recognized him as one. 'When they saw that I had been entrusted with the gospel to the uncircumcised ... and when they perceived the grace that was given to me, James and Cephas and John, who were reputed to be pillars, gave to me and Barnabas the right hand of fellowship' (Gal. 2.7–9). Paul showed in this letter that people are put right with God by faith, not by keeping the Jewish law. In case anyone should misunderstand his teaching about the law, Paul described what life in the Spirit was like, and listed the fruit of the Spirit (Gal. 5.13–14, 22).

Galatians is a rather angry letter. In it Paul defended himself, and attacked the people who were attacking his teaching.

Philippians

Paul's letter to the Philippians is a thank-you letter. He wrote it when he was in prison, not knowing whether he would be released or executed (Phil. 1.12–14; 2.17). The Christians of Philippi had sent Paul presents before. This time they had sent them with a man called Epaphroditus. When Epaphroditus was ready to return to Philippi, Paul wrote this letter of thanks for him to take.

The gifts had been an encouragement to Paul, 'a fragrant offering, a sacrifice pleasing and acceptable to God' (Phil. 4.18). That may be part of the reason why Paul's letter to the Philippians is so full of joy and confidence. The Philippian Church was facing difficulties too, but this letter is full of loving encouragement and confidence in Jesus Christ. Paul could even see that God was using his imprisonment as a way of spreading the gospel.

4 LESS PERSONAL LETTERS TO PARTICULAR CHURCHES

Colossians

Colossae was a city near Ephesus in Asia Minor. Paul did not know the Colossian Christians personally, but he felt a responsibility for them, since the gospel had first been preached in Colossae by one of his fellow-workers.

There were some false teachers in the Colossian Church, who claimed to be superior to the others and to have had special visions. They had taught the Colossian Christians that they had to keep various laws, including circumcision, food laws, and special festivals: 'Let no one disqualify you ... taking his stand on visions, puffed up without reason by his sensuous mind ... Why do you submit to regulations,

"Do not handle, Do not taste, Do not touch," according to human precepts and doctrines?' (Col. 2.18, 20–22).

Paul wrote about what Jesus Christ had done by dying, and explained that Christians had come to fullness of life in Jesus. He described the new life in Christ, and explained briefly what it meant to be a Christian wife, husband, child, parent, slave or master.

Some biblical scholars believe that the letter to the Colossians was not written by Paul. They argue that the style of this letter (and that of the letter to the Ephesians) is very different from that of Paul's other letters. This leads them to think that these two letters were written later by another Christian leader, who had been deeply influenced by Paul, and who wrote them as if they were from Paul. In those days to use the name of an earlier author was not thought of as fraud, as it would be today. It was a mark of respect for a great man to write something in his name.

Ephesians

Paul had lived and worked in Ephesus for three years (Acts 20.31), and it does seem strange that he should have written such an impersonal letter to a Church which he knew well. The letter to the Ephesians hardly contains any personal greetings at all (see p. 88). The only name in it is that of Tychicus, who was to carry the letter (Eph. 6.21).

But Paul, or whoever wrote the letter, was not writing a personal letter. It was a pastoral letter, intended to be read aloud in different Churches. In some of the most ancient copies of the New Testament Ephesus is not mentioned at all (see RSV note a, and the chapter on Texts in volume 2). Maybe Tychicus was meant to read the letter aloud to all the Churches he visited on his way.

In fact the letter to the Ephesians is hardly a letter at all. It is a deep theological document about God's plan for the unity of all creation in Jesus Christ. The writer uses picture-language to describe the union of Jesus Christ with the Church. The Church is like a body, with Jesus as the head. It is like a building, with Jesus as the cornerstone. It is like a wife, with Jesus as her husband (Eph. 4.12–16; 2.20–22; 5.22–32). The letter appeals to Christians to show their unity with Christ in the way they live.

Romans

Paul had not founded the Church in Rome, nor even visited the Christians there. He was hoping to visit them soon, and then to go on to Spain (Rom. 15.22–24). The letter is the longest of Paul's New Testament letters. It is not related to any particular problem which the Church in Rome was facing.

In Romans Paul set out his understanding of the Christian faith, and

The letters of Timothy and Titus describe the sort of people who should be appointed leaders in the Church – people like these theological students at a lecture in Tanzania. In Paul's time most theological teaching was by word of mouth, or through letters like Romans and Ephesians. Today so many works of theology are published that librarians – as at the Union Seminary in the Philippines – continually have new consignments of books to catalogue.

how it worked out in everyday life. With the exception of chapter 16, the letter to the Romans is a general theological document. Paul explained the basis of his faith, with the result that this letter has been described as 'the gospel according to Paul'. He showed how all mankind was under the power of sin. The only way to be put right with God was through faith in Jesus Christ: 'For there is no distinction; since all have sinned and fall short of the glory of God, they are justified by his grace as a gift, through the redemption which is in Christ Jesus, whom God put forward as an expiation by his blood, to be received by faith' (Romans 3.22–25).

Paul dealt with the place of the Jewish law, and the place of the Spirit, in the life of a believer. As a Jew himself he tried to explain the part which the Jewish people had in God's plan. Finally, he wrote about the practical matters of living as a Christian, including the question of a Christian's duty to the state.

Chapter 16, however, is full of personal greetings. Since Rome was the centre of the Roman Empire it seems likely that Paul, who was himself a Roman citizen, knew a lot of people there. On the other hand, some scholars think that Chapter 16 was originally part of a letter sent to Ephesus.

STUDY SUGGESTIONS

WORDS AND MEANINGS

1. What does the word 'pastoral' usually mean when it is used by Christians? What does its use as a title lead you to expect about the Letters studied in this chapter? John 21.15–18 may help you to answer this question.

REVIEW OF CONTENT

2. Which letters are called the 'Pastoral Letters'?
3. Which runaway slave caused Paul to write a letter, and what was the result of their meeting?
4. Where was Paul when he wrote to the Philippians? What reasons did he have to be joyful when he wrote it?
5. What is the main reason why a number of biblical scholars believe that Colossians and Ephesians were not written by Paul?
6. What seems to be missing:
   (a) from some ancient manuscripts of Ephesians?
   (b) from Ephesians as a whole?

BIBLE STUDY

7. Look up Titus 1.7 in as many different Bible versions as you can,

and list the various words used instead of 'bishop' (RSV) to translate the Greek *'episcopos'*.

8. What did Paul ask Philemon to do which shows us that Paul was hoping to visit him soon?
9. Use a concordance to find some evidence in Paul's *other* letters that Timothy and Titus were his companions.
10. Read Philippians 1.27–30; 3.2–3; 4.1–3, and then describe two of the problems that seem to have been facing the Church in Philippi.
11. Read Colossians 1.1–8 and 4.7–17. What was the name of Paul's fellow-worker who had first preached in Colossae, and where was he when Paul wrote this letter?
12. What picture-language showing the relationship of Jesus and the Church is to be found in Ephesians and in 1 Corinthians? Give the references.

FURTHER STUDY AND DISCUSSION

13. How would you answer someone who asked you to explain why the letters studied in this chapter are called 'Pastoral'?
14. Paul declared that 'there is neither Jew nor Greek, there is neither slave nor free, there is neither male nor female; for you are all one in Christ Jesus' (Gal. 3.28). What controversy led him to make this great affirmation? What do you consider to be its meaning for the Church today?
15. Paul wrote to the Roman Church about a Christian's duty to the state (Romans 13.1–7). Why did he write on this topic to the Romans? What practical application does his teaching have for the Church in your country today? What practical application does it have for you as an individual?
16. Why was the question of circumcision an important one for Paul? Is this a matter which has any importance in your community? If so, what difference, if any, does Paul's teaching make to the situation?

EIGHT MORE LETTERS

THREE LETTERS OF JOHN

There are three letters which according to tradition were written by John the son of Zebedee. 2 and 3 John, which are both very short, begin with the words 'The Elder to . . .'. 1 John is longer, and does not begin like a letter at all. Many scholars doubt whether the 'Elder' was the same person as John the son of Zebedee. Some argue that the Gospel of John, the letters of John, and the Revelation of John were written by three different people.

1 John

1 John does not start by saying who is writing or to whom he is writing. However it does appear that the author knew the people he was writing to: he called them 'my children' and 'my dear friends'. 1 John could be a pastoral letter from a leader to a group of Churches for whom he had a responsibility. His reason for writing was that false teachers had attacked his teaching. These teachers said that Jesus was not the Christ, that He had not come as a human being. They claimed to know God, but they did not keep His commandments. They claimed to be 'in the light', but they did not show love for their Christian brothers. Recently the false teachers had left the Church.

The letter was written to reassure the readers. The writer encouraged them to live in true fellowship with God, and warned about false teaching which could destroy that fellowship. There are many similarities between 1 John and the Fourth Gospel.

2 John

2 John is a letter from 'the Elder' to 'the elect lady and her children'. Probably this is some sort of disguise, and the letter is actually to a Church and its members. The final greeting, 'the children of your elect sister greet you', is probably a greeting from the Church to which the letter-writer belonged. 2 John is so short that it is a note rather than a letter. It warns that there are false teachers going around, probably the same false teachers mentioned in 1 John. They were 'men who will not acknowledge the coming of Jesus Christ in the flesh' (2 John 7). The writer says that false teachers should not be made welcome or be helped in any way.

3 John

3 John was written by 'the Elder' to Gaius. He praised Gaius for the way he had helped visiting Christians in the past, and asked him to give more help (3 John 5–6). Diotrephes, a leader in Gaius's Church, did not acknowledge the Elder's authority and was causing some problems, but there is no hint that he was teaching false doctrine. The Elder hoped to see Gaius soon.

HEBREWS

Hebrews is another New Testament letter which does not at first look like a letter. There are no opening greetings and no names, either of the writer or of the people to whom he was writing. The writer described it as a 'word of exhortation': 'I appeal to you, brethren, bear with my word of exhortation, for I have written to you briefly' (Heb. 13.22).

No one knows who wrote the letter to the Hebrews. The idea that

Paul wrote it is wrong, although the writer shows in his farewell greeting that he was a friend of Timothy. It was called the Letter to the Hebrews because it is full of Jewish ideas and quotations from the Jewish Scriptures.

In Hebrews Jesus is shown as the true High Priest: 'When Christ appeared as a high priest . . . he entered once for all into the Holy Place, taking not the blood of goats and calves but his own blood, thus securing an eternal redemption . . . Therefore he is the mediator of a new covenant . . . For Christ has entered not into a sanctuary made with hands, . . . but into heaven itself, now to appear in the presence of God on our behalf.' (Heb. 9.11–24.)

The writer was explaining what God had done, but he was explaining it to a particular group of people. He knew his readers well, and had known them for a long time: 'Recall the former days when, after you were enlightened, you endured a hard struggle with sufferings, sometimes being publicly exposed to abuse and affliction, and sometimes being partners with those so treated' (Heb. 10.32–33). It appears that the readers of the letter were in danger of being unfaithful to Jesus and drifting away from the Church. The letter is full of encouragement to stay faithful: 'Let us hold fast the confession of our faith without wavering' (Heb. 10.23). In particular they should remain faithful in the face of persecution: 'Consider him who endured from sinners such hostility against himself, so that you may not grow weary or faint-hearted. In your struggle against sin you have not yet resisted to the point of shedding your blood.' (Heb. 12.3–4.)

As in so many of the other New Testament Letters, the author was hoping soon to see the people to whom he was writing.

TWO LETTERS TO THE DISPERSION

'To the exiles of the Dispersion in Pontus, Galatia, Cappadocia, Asia, and Bithynia, chosen and destined by God the Father and sanctified by the Spirit for obedience to Jesus Christ and for sprinkling with his blood' (1 Peter 1.2).

We have already seen that many Jews lived outside Palestine, and were called the Jews of the Dispersion (p. 67). James and 1 Peter are both addressed to 'the Dispersion'. The opening verses of 1 Peter make clear that the writer was addressing his fellow Christians. The early Christians thought of themselves as being the 'new Israel'. Once the Church had spread beyond Palestine it was in dispersion, like the old Israel. However it was in dispersion in a deeper sense as well. All Christians were in the dispersion from the heavenly Jerusalem, which was their true home.

James seems to have written his letter for any scattered Christians. 1 Peter is addressed to the Christians of Asia Minor.

James

The writer of James is unlikely to have been James the son of Zebedee, who was executed by Herod Agrippa very early in the history of the Church. Another James, the brother of Jesus, became a leader of the Church in Jerusalem (cf. Gal. 1.19), and many scholars think it was he who wrote this letter. It is a collection of practical instructions about the right attitudes and behaviour for Christians. The letter contains no hint of any tension between Jews and Gentiles, which might mean that James wrote it very early, when there were few Gentile Christians.

James only mentions Jesus by name twice in the whole letter, but all through he echoes the teachings of Jesus. Like Jesus, James condemns the empty practice of religion: 'Faith apart from works is dead' (James 2.26). Some people have thought that James wrote this letter to disagree with Paul, who wrote, 'by grace you have been saved through faith' (Eph. 2.8). However James was only saying that faith has to show itself in the way that Christians live. Paul too believed this.

1 Peter

This letter was apparently written by Peter from Rome. 'She who is at Babylon, who is likewise chosen, sends you greetings' (1 Peter 5.13). In the book of Revelation 'Babylon' stands for Rome, and it probably means the same here. If Peter needed to disguise the place he was writing from, it could mean that the Christians there were facing persecution. There is no hint in the letter that the writer knew the readers, or that he had any plans to visit them. Some scholars have doubted whether Peter wrote this letter personally. They have argued that a disciple of Peter's wrote down Peter's teaching, perhaps even one of his sermons, in the form of a letter.

The main subject of the letter is suffering. The writer believed that the end of the world was near: 'The end of all things is at hand ... Beloved, do not be surprised at the fiery ordeal which comes upon you to prove you ... For the time has come for judgement to begin with the household of God' (1 Peter 4.7–17). The 'fiery ordeal' was one of the signs that the end was near (see chapter 8), so Peter was writing to other Christians to warn and encourage them. He reminded them of the hope and confidence which they had in God because of Jesus. They could be glad about suffering as Christians, because it was a chance to share in the sufferings of Jesus: 'Rejoice in so far as you share Christ's sufferings, that you may also rejoice and be glad when his glory is revealed' (1 Peter 4.13).

Like Paul's letters to Corinth, those of James, Peter, John and Jude warn against false teachers who invent stories, despise authority, and insist on having their own way. Again and again the Church has had to decide whether some of those claiming to speak in the name of God – like the 'Jesus-freaks' and drugs-and-love movements which drew great crowds in America, or the 'Scientology' Church offering personality tests in London – really are true, or false and dangerous.

TWO LETTERS ABOUT FALSE TEACHERS

2 Peter

2 Peter was apparently written by Peter, but it is completely different in style and content from 1 Peter. Many people doubt whether Peter himself wrote it. There is no mention in the letter of who it was written to, or where it was written from.

The main aim of this letter is to give a warning, but it is not a warning about persecution. The readers were in danger from false teachers, who made up stories, despised authority, and were immoral (2 Peter 1.16; 2.10; 2.12–15). They also doubted whether Jesus was going to return: 'You must understand this, that scoffers will come in the last days with scoffing ... saying, "Where is the promise of his coming?"' (2 Peter 3.4).

Jude

Jude claims to be a brother of James, but which James is not explained. The letter of Jude is very short, and we do not know to whom he was writing. The content and style of the letter are very similar to 2 Peter. Most of it is a warning about false teachers, 'ungodly persons who pervert the grace of our God into licentiousness and deny our only Master and Lord, Jesus Christ' (Jude 4). Jude sees the appearance of such people as a sign that the end of the age is near (Jude 18, and see p. 116).

STUDY SUGGESTIONS

WORDS AND MEANINGS

1. Explain the meaning of the following words:
   (a) 'reassure' (b) 'licentiousness' (c) 'scoffers'.
2. Who are 'the elect'?

REVIEW OF CONTENT

3. What did the writer of 2 and 3 John call himself?
4. What did the writer of Hebrews say his letter was?
5. What kinds of difficulty were the first readers of the Letter to the Hebrews facing?
6. How is it possible for Christians to be called 'the Dispersion'?
7. There are two men called James mentioned in the New Testament. Explain who they both were.
8. Name three New Testament letters which are concerned with false teachers.

BIBLE STUDY

9. Read 1 John 1.5—2.19. The author was writing about teachers who 'say' various things. Find four things which they seem to have been saying, according to this passage?
10. 1 John 3.7–10 explains how we may tell whether a teacher is a false teacher or not. Use the RSV footnotes to discover what words of Jesus give similar guidance.
11. Find the evidence in Hebrews that the writer was a friend of Timothy.
12. Read Hebrews 12.12. What does this verse tell us about the people to whom the letter was sent?
13. Use a concordance to discover some words of Jesus (and give their references) which are very like these verses of James:

    (a) 'Has not God chosen those who are poor in the world to be rich in faith and heirs of the kingdom which he has promised to those who love him?' (James 2.5).

    (b) 'Can a fig tree, my brethren, yield olives, or a grapevine figs?' (James 3.12).

    (c) 'There is one lawgiver and judge, he who is able to save and to destroy. But who are you that you judge your neighbour?' (James 4.12).

    (d) 'Your riches have rotted and your garments are moth-eaten. Your gold and silver have rusted . . . You have laid up treasure for the last days' (James 5.2–3).

14. Which 'faithful brother' wrote down 1 Peter?
15. Find the Old Testament passage on which 1 Peter 2.9 is based. How many similarities can you find between the two passages?
16. To which Jewish practices was the writer of the Letter to the Hebrews referring in 9.11–24.

FURTHER STUDY AND DISCUSSION

17. Some Churches emphasize 'the priesthood of all believers' (see 1 Peter 2.4–9). What effect do you think this has on their individual members? What do you yourself understand by the phrase, and how far do you find it helpful?
18. 1 John describes several ways in which false teachers can be 'tested' and identified. What are those ways? Which of the 'tests' do you consider to be the most important?

    Following John's suggestions, which people or groups of people, if any, in your own experience would you regard as 'false teachers'?

8

Eschatology:
The Doctrine of the Last Things

THE DAY OF THE LORD

'The Day of the Lord will come like a thief in the night'
(1 Thess. 5.2).

JEWISH BELIEFS

Two Ages

The Jews believed that there were two 'ages' of time, 'this present age' in which we live, and 'the age to come'. They expected God to appear in glory on 'the Day of the Lord', when He would bring the present age to an end and conquer all His enemies. The Day of the Lord would be a day of judgement and destruction, but it would be followed by the age to come, a time of righteousness, peace and prosperity for the Jews.

Some Jews believed that there would be yet another period of time in between the two ages. Some thought it would last for forty years, others thought it would be 400 years. The Revelation refers to an in-between period of 1,000 years, known as the 'millennium'. Mixed up with ideas of 'the age between' was the idea of a Messiah. Some Jews thought that the Messiah would rule during the in-between period.

Apocalyptic Writing

'Eschatology' includes every kind of teaching about the 'last things', i.e. death, judgement, heaven, hell, etc. (see Glossary). Much of it is found in apocalyptic writings, which are especially about the last day and the events surrounding it. Apocalyptic means 'unveiling', making something plain. An apocalyptic book, which may also be called an 'apocalypse', is intended to reveal what is going to happen in the future.

A Result of Persecution

Nearly 200 years before the time of Jesus a Syrian king called Antiochus Epiphanes ruled Palestine, and tried to wipe out the Jewish religion. He burned the holy books, forbade circumcision, and ordered the Jews to eat pork and sacrifice to Greek gods. Many Jews refused to obey, and as a result they were tortured and killed.

It seemed that the world was under the control of Satan. God did not appear to be in charge of the nations, or to be keeping His promises to the Jewish people. In this situation Jewish apocalyptic writing began and flourished. The book of Daniel in the Old Testament is an apocalyptic book which was almost certainly written during the persecution by Antiochus Epiphanes.

Jewish apocalyptic writing continued to flourish until the end of the first century AD. The basic ideas it contained were:

1. That this age is ruled by Satan and the forces of evil;
2. That God will act when things seem at their worst, and bring in the age to come;
3. That the outcome of events is already fixed in heaven. All we have to do is just remain faithful.

JESUS'S TEACHING

'I am with you always, to the close of the age' (Matt. 28.20). We cannot tell exactly what Jesus believed about the last things. His teaching was often in pictures, parables and riddles, and He left people to puzzle out the meaning for themselves. But some of the things that the Gospel writers understood Jesus to have taught are fairly clear.

1. Jesus referred to 'the last day', which would be a day of resurrection and judgement (see John 6.40).

2. Matthew, Mark and Luke all record words of Jesus about 'the day of judgement', 'the judgement' and 'on that day'.

3. The Gospels record words of Jesus about the 'Son of man' coming to be the judge (Matt. 16.27; Mark 8.30; Luke 12.8; cf. John 5.27).

4. Jesus claimed that even He Himself did not know when 'that day' would be: 'But of that day or that hour no one knows, not even the angels in heaven, nor the Son, but only the Father' (Mark 13.32). Many of the sayings in the Gospels suggest that it would come suddenly, without warning (cf. Matt. 25.13; Mark 13.34–37; Luke 21.34).

5. Several Gospel passages refer to a period of distress that would apparently come immediately before the last day: 'For in those days there will be such tribulation as has not been from the beginning of creation which God created until now, and never will be. ... But in those days, after that tribulation, the sun will be darkened, and the moon will not give its light ... And then they will see the Son of man coming in clouds with great power and glory.' (Mark 13.19, 24–26 and parallel passages in Matthew and Luke.)

THE BELIEF OF THE EARLY CHURCH

'The times of ignorance God overlooked, but now he commands all men everywhere to repent, because he has fixed a day on which he will judge the world in righteousness by a man whom he has appointed' (Acts 17.30–31). Following Jewish belief and the teaching of Jesus, Christians have always believed that there would be a 'last day', when

The Jews expected a Day of Judgement when God would bring the present age to an end. The Gospels too refer to a time of warfare and tribulation 'at the close of the age' when 'the sun will be darkened and the moon not give its light'. Ever since the first atomic bomb was dropped, some people have believed that, as scientists have confirmed, nuclear war could indeed result in the sun being hidden long enough to bring most if not all life on earth to an end. And some well-known Christians have been foremost in campaigning for nuclear disarmament, such as Bruce Kent (centre), leading this group of demonstrators to join a protest march against siting nuclear missiles in Britain.

Jesus would return in glory to judge the world. The theological term for Jesus's second coming is '*parousia*', a Greek word meaning 'coming' or 'arrival'. The return of Jesus as Judge and Saviour was a part of the kerygma (see p. 61).

It seems that the early Christians expected Jesus to return soon, and they waited impatiently for the day to come. We have already seen how some of the Thessalonian Christians gave up their jobs because they thought Jesus was about to return. Other Christians were impatient too: 'Be patient therefore, brethren, until the coming (*parousia*) of the Lord. Behold, the farmer waits for the precious fruit of the earth, being patient over it until he receives the early and the late rain. You also be patient. Establish your hearts, for the coming of the Lord is at hand.' (James 5.7–8.)

When persecution and suffering had to be endured, Christians accepted it as a sign that they were living in the last days (see 2 Tim. 3.1). The gift of the Spirit was seen as one of the signs of this (Acts 2.17). God had already acted: 'in these last days he has spoken to us by a Son' (Heb. 1.2). When Christians were persecuted it was seen as a sign that the end was very near.

STUDY SUGGESTIONS

WORDS AND MEANINGS

1. Give a brief explanation of each of the following words:
   (a) eschatology   (b) apocalyptic   (c) parousia
2. Find another way of expressing the phrase: 'immediately before the last day'.

REVIEW OF CONTENT

3. In which centuries did Jewish apocalyptic writing flourish?
4. Which Old Testament book is an apocalyptic book?
5. Give the name and the nationality of the king who persecuted the Jews in Palestine in the second century BC.
6. What are some of the signs which are expected to show that the last days have arrived?

BIBLE STUDY

7. Use a concordance to find two passages in the Revelation which refer to the day of God's judgement as coming 'like a thief'. What is the chief difference between the two passages?
8. In each of the following passages in John's Gospel Jesus speaks of the last day. What particular messages about the last day do these various passages contain? (a) John 6.40 (b) 11.17–27 (c) 12.47–48.

9. Compare Matt. 10.15 and 11.22 with Luke 10.12, 14. What expressions does Luke use where Matthew uses 'day of judgement'?
10. Read Amos 5.18–20. Why did the Israelites hope for the day of the Lord, and why did Amos say they should fear it instead?
11. Apocalyptic writing often contains visions of strange animals which stand for historical people. Read Daniel 8.1–27, and then say who the following animals and parts of animals represent:
   (a) the ram with two horns,
   (b) the he-goat with a conspicuous horn between his eyes,
   (c) the 'little horn, which grew exceedingly great'.

FURTHER STUDY AND DISCUSSION

12. The early Christians expected Jesus to return *soon*. What are the good and the bad effects of such a belief?
13. In both the Apostle's Creed and the Nicene Creed Christians state: 'I believe in . . . Jesus Christ . . . He will come again . . . to judge the living and the dead.'

   Why are these statements a part of our creeds? What do you yourself think and feel as you say these words? Do you think all other Christians think and feel the same as you do? If you can, discuss this with fellow Church members, and consider with them the importance or unimportance of any differences which there may be between different people's thoughts and feelings.
14. Ever since the time of Jesus, Christians have been seeing 'signs' that the end of the world was near. What are some of these signs? In what other ways do you think those signs might be interpreted?

THE APOCALYPSE OF JOHN

The New Testament contains one apocalypse, also called 'The Revelation to John', or most commonly 'Revelation'. (NB: 'Revelation' is singular. There is no 's' on the end.)

AN APOCALYPTIC LETTER

'John, to the seven churches that are in Asia: Grace to you and peace . . .' (Rev. 1.4). At first sight it might appear that the Revelation is just another *letter*, written by a man called John to a group of Churches. Chapters 2 and 3 contain the names of the seven towns where those Churches were. Yet a closer look at Revelation shows us that it is no ordinary letter; it is an apocalyptic letter.

The Church began in a time when Jewish apocalyptic literature was popular, so that it was natural for Christians to use apocalyptic ideas and forms, especially in a time of persecution. Revelation shares many of the characteristics of Jewish apocalyptic writing. John describes what he has seen in visions, and he uses strange pictures and symbolic language. The simple message at the heart of Revelation is this: 'The end is very near. We are living in terrifying times, and things will get worse. Be brave and faithful to the end, and when Jesus comes He will reward you.'

THE WRITER

The style of writing in the Revelation is quite different from that of the Gospel or the Letters of John. This probably means that a different John wrote Revelation, although possibly the same man used a totally different style when writing an apocalypse.

Clearly the writer had seen and experienced terrible suffering, which made him cry out for vengeance. He writes of 'rivers of blood' (cf. Rev. 14.20) and describes the city of Rome as a 'harlot' who was 'drunk with the blood of the saints and the blood of the martyrs of Jesus' (Rev. 17.6). John says of himself that he has shared 'in Jesus the tribulation and the kingdom and the patient endurance'. Apparently he received his visions on the island of Patmos, where he was 'on account of the word of God and the testimony of Jesus' (Rev. 1.9). Patmos is a rocky little island about ten miles long and five miles wide, forty miles off the coast of Turkey. The Romans used such islands as places to send political prisoners, so John may have been sent there because he was a Christian.

ROMAN PERSECUTION OF CHRISTIANS

The first severe persecution of Christians by the Romans was in AD 64–65 under the Emperor Nero. In AD 64 a terrible fire burned in Rome for six days, and destroyed a large part of the city. According to the Roman historian Tacitus, many people believed that Nero himself had ordered the fire to be started. To put an end to the rumours, Nero blamed the fire on the Christians. Those who admitted that they were Christians were arrested and charged with 'hatred of the human race'. Tacitus records that great numbers were convicted and killed. Some were torn to pieces by dogs. Others were 'fastened on crosses, and, when daylight failed, were burned to serve as lamps by night'. Nero mixed with the crowds and enjoyed the dreadful sight. The persecution was so terrible that some Romans began to pity the Christians, and to feel 'that they were being sacrificed ... to the ferocity of a single man'.

The persecution ended with Nero's death. However, the Roman authorities had learned to distinguish Christians from Jews. Christianity was not a 'religio licita' (see p. 22), and was not granted the status of a permitted religion until 300 years after the crucifixion.

For the Romans the worship of the Roman gods was seen as necessary for state security. Half a century after Nero the Emperor Trajan wrote to the governor of Bithynia who had asked for his advice about how to deal with Christians. Trajan told the governor not to hunt out Christians. If people were charged with being Christian they should have a chance to deny it. If they proved they were not, by offering prayer to the Roman gods, they were to be pardoned. But if any admitted to being Christians the governor was right to execute them.

EMPEROR-WORSHIP

Centuries earlier the Persians had worshipped their rulers, and the practice spread to Rome from the East. In AD 14, when the Emperor Augustus died, the Roman Senate declared that he had become a god, and they continued this practice for the next seventy years. When in AD 88 the Emperor Domitian demanded to be addressed as 'Lord and god', most people accepted it. From that time onwards the worship of the Emperor became an important part of the state religion. But of course true Christians could not worship either the Roman gods or the Emperor.

CHRISTIANS AND THE STATE

We find different attitudes towards the state expressed in different parts of the New Testament. Most of the New Testament writers approved of Roman rule. Although the Romans executed Jesus, the New Testament writers preferred to put the blame on the Jews. In the Gospels and in Acts we read about several just and good Roman officials. Paul was proud to be a Roman citizen, and told the Christians in Rome to accept the authority of the government as being given by God. The teaching of 1 Peter is very similar.

In the Revelation we find a totally different approach to the state. The demand that people should worship the Emperor, and the persecution of Christians, had changed the whole situation. For the writer of Revelation the Emperor was a 'beast', the servant of Satan, the 'great dragon'. 'The great dragon . . . who is called the devil and Satan . . . was thrown down to earth. And I saw a beast rising out of the sea . . . and to it the dragon gave his power and his throne and great authority. Men worshipped the dragon . . . and they worshipped the beast, saying, "Who is like the beast, and who can fight against it?" And the beast was allowed to make war on the saints and to conquer them' (Rev. 12.9; 13.1–7).

John must have written the Revelation at some time between the persecution by Nero and the reign of Trajan. Most biblical scholars think he wrote it during the reign of Domitian.

PERSECUTION STILL TO COME

John had experienced persecution, yet clearly the Churches to whom he was writing had not experienced it to the same extent. Persecution was still in the future for them: 'Because you have kept my word of patient endurance, I will keep you from the hour of trial which is coming on the whole world' (Rev. 3.10). Probably John believed that the persecution which he had seen and suffered was going to spread to the rest of the Roman Empire. He was writing to his friends in Asia Minor to prepare them for the terrors that might be in store, and to encourage them to hold firm to their faith.

JOHN'S VISIONS

John's method of preparing his friends was to describe to them a series of visions:

1. John's first vision is of the risen Christ, who appears in dazzling clothes and commands John to write down His messages to the seven Churches (Rev. 1.12—3.22).

2. After that John seems to go through a door into heaven. He is in God's throne-room, where the inhabitants of heaven constantly worship and praise God (Rev. 4.1—5.14).

3. In the remainder of the book John is sometimes watching what is happening in heaven, and sometimes watching events on earth.

In heaven John sees God and the worship of God. He sees Jesus as a lamb, as the crowned Son of man on a cloud, and as a rider on a white horse. He watches the war in heaven, and sees Satan and his angels thrown down to earth.

On earth John sees terror and destruction on all sides. He sees the destruction of a great part of the Temple in Jerusalem, and the fall of 'the great city ... Babylon' (Rev. 16.19), which stands for Rome.

4. John's final and best known vision is of a new heaven and a new earth (Rev. 21.1—22.5). He sees a new Jerusalem coming down from heaven. In that city there is no mourning, no pain, no death. God is the city's light, and the city's gates are open for ever. All those who have been faithful to Jesus can go in, but nothing impure, no one who practises falsehood, is allowed inside.

SYMBOLS

The Revelation is the most difficult book of the New Testament to understand. More than any other New Testament book it is full of picture-language which is not meant to be taken literally. For example, Jesus is pictured in Rev. 5.6 as a lamb with seven horns and seven eyes! Seven was a number which symbolized perfection. Horns symbolized power and eyes symbolized knowledge. When John described Jesus in this way he was saying that Jesus had complete power and knowledge.

'John believed the persecution was going to spread. He wrote to prepare his friends, to comfort and encourage them.' In many countries today there are Christians and others who suffer persecution, like the priest Jerzy Popieluszko, murdered for upholding human rights in Poland. And there are people who warn and comfort the sufferers, like the parish clergy in Chile holding special vigils to pray for men detained or 'disappeared' in police and army terror raids, and denouncing government violence against innocent victims.

To study Revelation is a rewarding experience, providing that we read it with the help of a good commentary to guide us through its symbolism (there is a TEF Guide to Revelation). Without such help most of us are in danger of misunderstanding and misusing the letter. John wrote it to people who were used to apocalyptic writing and would understand it. He wrote it to comfort and encourage Christians of his own time, and like the other New Testament writers, he did not think that he was writing 'Scripture'.

STUDY SUGGESTIONS

WORDS AND MEANINGS

1. Explain the meaning of: (a) 'vengeance'　(b) 'a harlot'　(c) 'symbolic language'
2. What does 'distinguish' mean in the sentence: 'The Romans had learned to distinguish between Jews and Christians'?

REVIEW OF CONTENT

3. The four Roman Emperors mentioned in this chapter are Augustus, Nero, Domitian and Trajan. Which one of them:
(a) demanded to be addressed as 'Lord and god'?
(b) agreed that anyone who admitted to being a Christian should be executed?
(c) took pleasure in watching Christians burn on crosses?
(d) was declared at his death to have become a god?
4. What do we know about Patmos, and what was the possible reason for John's being there?

BIBLE STUDY

5. What kind of book is Revelation, according to its writer? (See Rev. 22.10; cf. 1.3; 22.18.)
6. Name three 'good Romans' who are mentioned in Acts.
7. What does the writer of 1 Peter say about the Emperor?
8. Find out the significance of the following numbers in the Bible generally, and in Revelation in particular: 3, 4, 7, 6, 12.
9. What is symbolized by 'the hundred and forty-four thousand who had been redeemed from the earth' (Rev. 14.3; cf. 7.4).

FURTHER STUDY AND DISCUSSION

10. What do you think is the proper attitude for Christians to have towards the governing authorities of their country?
What situations have you experienced in your own country, in

which you do not feel that you can give to the state all that it demands from you?

In which countries of the world today do you think it would be: (a) more difficult, and (b) easier, to be a Christian than in most other countries, and for what reasons?

10. What, if any, organizations, societies, or political parties do you know of, which you consider demand the sort of total loyalty which Christians cannot give to anyone except God? What are their demands which make you feel that way about them?

11. Today the word 'citizen' usually means an 'inhabitant' of a large city, e.g. 'the citizens of Bombay' – or Hong Kong or Nairobi or New York means the people who live in those places. Find out what it meant to be a 'Roman citizen' in New Testament times, and so, why Paul was proud to be one.

12. In the time of Nero Christians were charged with 'hatred of the human race'. What 'offence', if any may a Christian, whose only crime is following Jesus, be accused of today: (a) in your country? (b) in other countries? Why do you think that some rulers are reluctant to say it is a crime to be a Christian?

13. If you, or people you know, have actually suffered persecution on account of being Christian, what chiefly enabled you or them to stand firm? What help and support if any did you receive from the leaders of your Church? from other individual Christians?

14. In some countries today Christians are treated with contempt and even ridicule, though not actually persecuted. Which do you think is most likely to weaken a person's faith, ridicule or persecution, and why?

THE RETURN OF JESUS

There are references to the parousia of Jesus (see Glossary) and the end of the world in many of the New Testament books, besides the ones we have noted.

HOW SOON WILL IT BE?

In Paul's letters we can see a change in how soon he expected the parousia to happen. When Paul wrote 1 Thessalonians he expected that he would still be alive when Jesus returned: 'The dead in Christ will rise first; then we who are alive, who are left, shall be caught up together with them in the clouds to meet the Lord in the air' (1 Thess. 4.16–17).

When he wrote to the Philippians from prison, however, he thought he might die before the parousia came, although he still expected it: 'I

Jesus's followers knew – and know – from their own experience that He was – and is – alive and present with them. They were – as Christians today are – already living in the 'new age', as witness the crowds who gather year after year to celebrate Christmas in the Church of the Nativity in Bethlehem.

am sure that he who began a good work in you will bring it to completion at the day of Jesus Christ' (Phil. 1.6). At that time Paul was in danger of being executed for his faith. He explained that whether the authorities released him or executed him, either situation would be a deliverance. 'To live is Christ and to die is gain' (Phil. 1.21). But there is no suggestion in Philippians that Paul expected to be set free by the return of Jesus. Probably he no longer expected Jesus to return during his lifetime.

WHY IS IT DELAYED?

Clearly some Christians were troubled by the fact that the day of the Lord had not yet arrived. Some were scoffing: 'Scoffers will come, following their own passions and saying, "Where is the promise of his coming? For ever since the fathers fell asleep, all things have continued as they were from the beginning of creation"' (2 Peter 3.3–4).

It appears from the closing verses of John's Gospel that some Christians had expected Jesus to return before the death of 'the beloved disciple' (see the chapter on the Gospel of John in Volume 2). When that disciple died and Jesus had still not returned, their faith was shaken. The editor of the Gospel was careful to point out that Jesus had not been making promises. He had been telling Peter to mind his own business: 'The saying spread abroad among the brethren that this disciple was not to die; yet Jesus did not say to him that he was not to die, but, "If it is my will that he remain until I come, what is that to you?"' (John 21.23).

SOME RE-THINKING

Christians began to re-think Jesus's teaching. Perhaps they had been wrong when they expected the parousia to happen quickly. They still expected Jesus to return, but they remembered other things which He had said. Jesus had taught that the kingdom of God was already present in Him: 'Now after John [i.e. the Baptist] was arrested, Jesus came into Galilee, preaching the gospel of God, and saying, "The time is fulfilled, and the kingdom of God is at hand"' (Mark 1.14). Jesus's followers realized that in some sense He had already returned. He had appeared to a number of His disciples after the crucifixion. More important still, they knew from their experience that He was alive and present with them. Joel's prophecy that the spirit of God would be poured out 'in the last days' had been fulfilled (see Joel 2.27–29).

The old age had ended with the coming of Jesus, and Christians were already living in the new age. Although the day of judgement was still to come, Christians could draw near to God now: 'Since we have confidence to enter the sanctuary by the blood of Jesus, by the new and living way which he opened for us through the curtain ... let us draw near with a true heart in full assurance of faith . . . and all the more as you see the Day drawing near' (Heb. 10.19–25).

The doctrine that the last things have already happened is called 'realized eschatology'. That idea is given its fullest expression in the Gospel of John: 'Truly, truly, the hour is coming and now is, when the dead will hear the voice of the Son of God, and those who hear will live' (John 5.25).

WRITING GOSPELS

As long as the *parousia* was expected very soon, perhaps the next day, perhaps the following week or following month, Christians did not need to write much down. When it was delayed, the situation changed. The fact that Jesus did not return was one of the reasons for writing the Gospels. There were other reasons as well. We shall look at the Gospels in Volume 2.

STUDY SUGGESTIONS

WORDS AND MEANINGS

1. How would you describe a 'scoffer'?

REVIEW OF CONTENT

2. Name three of the New Testament letters in which the writer discusses the day of the Lord.
3. (a) In which of Paul's letters did he clearly show that he expected to be alive when Jesus returned?
   (b) In which of his letters did he show that he thought he might be executed?
4. What connection was there between the 'beloved disciple' and the parousia?
5. Explain the meaning of 'realized eschatology'.

BIBLE STUDY

6. What reasons did the writer of 2 Peter give for the delay in Jesus's return?
7. Read Jeremiah 29.1–10.
   (a) How many years did Jeremiah tell the exiles that they would have to remain in Babylon?
   (b) What sort of things did God want them to do during those years?
8. Read the letters to the Churches in Ephesus and Laodicea in Rev. 2.1–7 and 3.15–22. What problems did those Churches apparently have? What difference, if any, would John's message that Jesus was about to return make to them?

FURTHER STUDY AND DISCUSSION

9. From time to time one group of Christians or another announces that the world will end on a certain date. What is your response to such an announcement?
10. What would be the advantages and what would be the disadvantages of knowing that the world was going to end in a few months?
11. Many people today believe that the world will end in nuclear war. Some even see the words of Jesus according to Matthew 24.29, and of several Old Testament passages, as directly foretelling the 'nuclear winter' that scientists say would result from it.
   What do you think should be the attitude of Christians towards-nuclear warfare? In the light of Jesus' words in Mark 12.13–17 and similar passages, what do you think should be the attitude of the Church towards governments which make (and sell) nuclear armaments?
12. All life on earth is threatened by the misuse of our environment, from cutting down trees for firewood to the careless use of chemicals. In many parts of the world today 'the ground is dismayed' (Jer. 14.4). Read Jer. 14.1–10, and consider how far this situation may be God's judgement on humankind for the selfish way we treat His creation.

Appendixes

1. GLOSSARY OF TECHNICAL TERMS

ALLEGORY: A method of teaching or expressing ideas by telling a story or showing a picture in which various details stand for something else, e.g. the story of the wicked tenants (Mark 12.1–11).

APOCALYPSE (APOCALYPTIC): A book claiming to reveal heavenly secrets about the coming of God's kingdom, which is expected soon.

APOSTLE: Literally, 'someone who is sent' (from the Greek title for an ambassador or messenger). The name was given to the twelve disciples after the resurrection. Paul used it to mean someone who was personally commissioned by the risen Christ. See John 20.21; Acts 1.8; Eph. 3.1–5.

ARAMAIC: The language which Palestinian Jews spoke in the time of Jesus.

CHRIST: The anointed one. '*Christos*' in Greek, '*Messiah*' in Hebrew. 'Christos' came to be used like a surname for Jesus – 'Jesus Christ'.

CIRCUMCISION: The removal by surgery of the foreskin of the penis. All Jewish boys were circumcised on the eighth day as a sign of being Jewish. 'The circumcised' means Jews. 'The circumcision party' (see e.g. Gal. 2.12) refers to Christian Jews who thought that all Christians should be circumcised and keep the Jewish law.

CONCORDANCE: An alphabetical list of words used in the Bible, giving the Books, chapters and verses where they occur – very useful for finding references.

DISCIPLE: A learner or a follower. Used especially of the followers of Jesus.

ESCHATOLOGY: The doctrine of the 'last things' (see p. 113).

EVANGELIST: Someone who carries good news, especially anyone who preaches the good news about Jesus. Also a person who writes a Gospel.

EXILE: The period of Jewish history, from c.587–538 BC, when many Jews were forced to live in Babylon.

GOSPEL: Good News, especially the good news about Jesus. Also a written account of Jesus' life, death and resurrection.

HELLENIST: (From *Hellas* = Greece.) A person who adopted the Greek way of life. In the New Testament it means a Greek-speaking Jew.

HERODIAN: A supporter of King Herod.

KERYGMA: Proclamation or preaching. Especially the announcement of what God has done in Jesus.

MANUSCRIPT: A document written by hand. Nowadays the 'manuscript' of a book may be typed, but the word is not used for anything already printed.

MESSIAH: A Hebrew word meaning the anointed one. The Jews were expecting God to send a messiah to save them from their enemies.

MINISTRY: Service. Jesus' 'ministry' was the period of His life when He wandered about with the disciples, serving people by teaching and healing them. The ministry of the Church is the service of all Christians.

PARABLE: A story or a picture with a meaning, a comparison or riddle.

PAROUSIA: Arrival or coming. Used especially to mean the Second Coming of Jesus as Judge and Saviour in the last days.

PASSION: Jesus' 'passion' means His suffering and death.

PAPYRUS: Paper made from reeds. The sheets were joined together to make a roll (see p. 82).

PHARISEE: A member of a Jewish religious group who placed great emphasis on keeping the Jewish law.

PROSELYTE: A Gentile who became a Jew, was circumcised, and was bound by the Jewish law.

RABBI: The Hebrew name for a teacher. Many rabbis were also Pharisees.

SADDUCEE: A member of a Jewish religious group closely associated with the worship of the Temple in Jerusalem.

SANHEDRIN: The Supreme Council of the Jews.

SCRIBE: A person who writes. In the New Testament it usually refers to a man who was also an expert in the Jewish law, as in 'scribes and Pharisees'.

SHEMA: The Jewish confession of faith. It is made up of three passages from the Law, but especially Deuteronomy 6.4–5.

TORAH: The Hebrew word for 'law', commonly used to mean the first five books of the Bible, or, more specifically, the Law which God gave to His people the Jews through Moses.

ZEALOT: A Jewish freedom-fighter against the Roman overlords in the first century AD.

2. COMMON ABBREVIATIONS

AD   *Anno Domini*, (Latin for 'in the year of the Lord') referring to the years after the birth of Jesus.

AV   Authorized Version (of the Bible).

a,b,c,   as in 'Luke 2.21a'. Used to divide up a verse when giving references: 'a' refers to the first half of the verse; 'b' refers to the second half of the verse; 'c' is only used when referring to the last part of a long verse.

b.   born, normally followed by the date of birth.

BC   Before Christ, referring to years before the birth of Christ.

BCE   Before the Common Era. (Used by Muslims to mean the same as BC.)

c.   *circa*, Latin for 'around', 'about', as in 'Papias, *c.*60–*c.*130'. Used when only the approximate time of an event is known, not the exact year or date.

CE	Common Era (the same as AD).
cf.	*confer*, Latin for 'compare'.
d.	died.
e.g.	*exempli gratia*, Latin for 'for example'.
etc.	*et cetera*, Latin for 'and so on'.
f, ff.	following (singular and plural). Used in references to mean 'and the following one or more of the items numbered'. In Bible references 'f' usually means 'and following verse or verses up to the end of sentence, 'ff' means up to the end of the paragraph (as in 'Rom. 9.10f; Acts 6.8ff'). In other books it normally refers to the following page(s), paragraph(s) or line(s), according to the item numbered.
ibid.	*ibidem*, Latin for 'in the same place'. This is a reference to a work that has just been referred to.
i.e.	*id est*, Latin for 'that is'.
JB	Jerusalem Bible.
LXX	Septuagint (see Volume 2).
MS	Manuscript (pl. MSS).
N.B.	*Nota bene*, Latin for 'note well', 'take good note of'.
NEB	New English Bible.
NT	New Testament.
op. cit.	*opere citato*, Latin for 'in the work cited'. Used when giving a reference to a book that has already been quoted.
OT	Old Testament.
pl.	plural.
q.v.	*quod vide*, Latin for 'which see'.
RSV	Revised Standard Version of the Bible.
s.	singular.
TEV	Today's English Version, also sometimes abbreviated as GNB, for the Good News Bible.
v, vv	Verse, verses.

Key to Study Suggestions

Where the key to a question is marked with an asterisk, see also the Glossary (pp. 128-129) as an additional check.

Chapter 1: Introduction (Pages 7–8)

1. (a) and (b) See p. 1, first paragraph.
2. See p. 3, Section on Jesus as the Word of God, para. 1.
3. See pp. 1 and 2, Section on That little word 'of'.
4. See pp. 2 and 3.
5. (a) and (b) See p. 5, Section on Jewish and Muslim Ideas about the Word of God.
   (c) See p. 3.
6. (a) See v. 1; (b) See v. 3; (c) See v. 4; (d) See vv. 4, 9; (e) See v. 14; (f) See v. 11; (g) See v. 14; (h) See v. 18.
7. In each case the writer could have meant Jesus Christ.
8. Different disciples remembered what Jesus had said slightly differently, or perhaps interpreted His meaning differently. See pp. 62–64 and Vol. 2.

Chapter 2: Jesus, His Land and His People (Pages 14–15)

1. (a) See p. 9, line 27.
3. See p. 9, para. 1.
4. (a) See p. 9, Section on The House.
   (b) See p. 9, Section on Food.
5. See p. 10, Section on Clothing.
6. (a) See p. 12, para. 1.
7. See pp. 12 and 13, Section on Sabbaths.
8. See p. 12, para. 3.
9. See pp. 13 and 14, Section on Languages.
10. See p. 13, para. 4.
11. See pp. 13–14.

Pages 21–22

1. See p. 20.*
4. (a) See p. 5, para. 2.*
   (b)–(e) See p. 19, Section on The Traditions of the Elders.

6. See pp. 15–16, Section on The Temple and Sacrifice.

7. See p. 17, last 5 lines.

8. and 9. See p. 17, Section on Priests and Scribes.

10. See p. 19, Section on Sanhedrin.

11. See p. 20, para. 2.

12. See vv. 8–9.

13. See v. 18.

14. They fasted and performed ritual washing.

Pages 26–27

3. and 4. See p. 22, Section on Roman Rule.

5. See p. 23, Section on Herod the Great.

6. and 7. See p. 24, Section on The Jewish War and the Fall of Jerusalem.

8. (a)–(b) See p. 23, Section on Herod's Sons.
   (c)–(f) See p. 24, Section on Herod Agrippa II.

9. (a) See p. 23, para. 2, lines 8–11.
   (b) and (c) See p. 23, para. 4.
   (d) See p. 23, last 3 lines.

11. See p. 24, Section on Samaritans.

Special Note A (Page 29)

2. See p. 28, para. 1, lines 5–7.

3. See p. 28, para. 2, line 1.

4. See p. 28, last paragraph.

5. When a new king began to reign in Judah the writer states which year it was in the reign of the King of Israel. In the same way, when a new king began to reign in Israel, he states which year it was in the reign of the King of Judah.

6. and 7. See List of Abbreviations, p. 129.

Chapter 3: Jesus the Teacher (Pages 35–36)

1. (a) See p. 32, Section on The Twelve.*
   (b) See p. 30, para. 1.*
   (c) See p. 34, para. 4.*

4. (a) and (b) See p. 32, Section on Jewish Teachers.

5. See pp. 32–34, Section on The Twelve.

6. (a) See p. 32, lines 7–2 from foot of page.

(b) See John 11.1–3.
(c) See p. 32, lines 4–8.
(d) See John 3.1–4 and p. 31, para. 2.
(e) See Luke 8.1–3 and p. 31, Section on Women Disciples.
(f) See p. 34, para. 3.

7. He was a married man, who shared a house with his brother Andrew, and his wife's mother. He was a fisherman, who owned his own boat, and was in partnership with his brother and James and John.

8. (b) The verses imply that Jesus's hearers were married men who owned property. They had left their homes and families to follow Him.

10. See vv. 17, 19.

Pages 43–45

5. See p. 36, Section on Jesus's Teaching Methods.

6. See pp. 36–37, Section on Parables and Allegory.*

7. See p. 41, Section on Use of the Old Testament.

8. See p. 42, last 3 lines, and p. 43.

9. (a) Make use of your opportunities.
   (b) What you do is more important than what you say.
   (c) Sinners are in a better position to receive from God than many 'religious' people.
   (d) The time to follow Christ is now.
   (e) The growth of the Kingdom is in God's hands.

10. See p. 40, Section on Parallelism in Hebrew Poetry.

11. See v. 7.

12. Perhaps it was a symbolic act of judgement.

Chapter 4: The Central Events (Pages 51–52)

1. See p. 46, last 3 lines.

4. (a) See p. 46, Section on Religious Reasons, especially lines 5–7 and 19–23.
   (b) See p. 47, Section on Political Reasons.

5. See p. 48, Section on The Romans' Part, lines 4–8.

6. See p. 50, last para.

9. See v. 16.

11. They still thought that Jesus was going to be an earthly ruler, see v. 37.

13. See p. 46, last para.

Pages 55–57

2. See p. 53, lines 9–16.

3. See p. 53–55, Section on The Disciples' Understanding.

5. (a) See vv. 3, 4.

Chapter 5: The Growth of the Church (Pages 65–66)

1. See p. 128.*

3. See p. 58, para. 2.

4. See p. 60, para. 4.

5. See p. 61, lines 26–41.

6. See p. 64, para. 4, lines 8–end and pp. 64–65, Section on The Work of the Church.

7. See p. 64, para 4, lines 4–6.

8. Good news.

10. (a) v. 7, breath of life; (b) v. 8, wind.

11. (a) In his speech in Athens Paul quotes from a Greek poet, but he does not quote from the Old Testament.
(b) His hearers in Athens were not Jews or God-fearers.

12. A Christian should be loyal to the State, but he is also answerable to God for everything that he does.

Pages 73–74

2. (a) See p. 68, para. 2.
(b) See p. 67, para. 2.
(c) See Glossary.

3. See pp. 67–68, Section on Proselytes and God-fearers.

4. See p. 69, Section on The First Gentile Christians.

5. See p. 67, last sentence.

6. See p. 72, para. 5.

7. See p. 69, para. 1

8. (a) See vv. 2, 22.
(b) See v. 28.
(d) See vv. 44–47.

9. They were Jewish Christians who believed that all Christians had to be circumcised and keep the Jewish law (See Act 15.1).

10. They all have Greek names.

Chapter 6: Writing Letters (Pages 80–81)

1. See p. 75, para. 2.
3. See p. 75, para. 3.
4. See p. 75, para. 1.
5. See p. 78, para. 2.
6. See p. 78, para. 6.
7. See p. 78, para. 2, and p. 81, last sentence.
8. See Matt. 24.43–44; Luke 12.39–40; 1 Thess. 5.2; 2 Peter 3.10; Rev. 3.3.
   (a) Jesus.
   (b) The Apostles followed Jesus's example, and used His illustrations.
9. They were dragged before the rulers, falsely accused, attacked by the crowd, and condemned to be stripped, beaten, imprisoned and fastened in the stocks.
10. See v. 1 'As you learned from me'; v. 2, 'You know what instructions we gave you'; v. 6 'as we solemnly forewarned you'; v. 11, 'as we charged you'.

Pages 85–86

3. (a) See p. 81, A Wife's Letter to her Husband, line 4.
   (b) See p. 82, line 1.
   (c) See p. 81, A Wife's Letter, lines 5–7, and p. 82, line 2.
4 and 5. See p. 82, Writing Materials.
6. See p. 81, para. 1.
7. (a) See Phil. 2.25,28.
   (b) See Phil. 4.18.
   (c) See Phil. 2.26–27.
8. Tychicus, see v. 21.
9. Paul wrote the last few sentences in his own handwriting, which implies that someone else had written the rest for him.
10. (a) See 1 Cor. 1.1.
    (b) See Philemon 1.
11. See Col. 4.8–9.

Page 90

2. See p. 88, Section on Editions, para. 4.
3. See p. 86, para. 1.
4. See p. 87, para. 3.
5. See p. 87, para. 4.

KEY TO STUDY SUGGESTIONS

6. See p. 87, last para.

7. See p. 88, Section on Editions.
(a) para. 1; (b) para. 2.

Special Note B; Cross References (Pages 91–92)

2. (a), (b) and (e).

5. See 2 Peter 1.17.

Chapter 7: New Testament Letters (Pages 98–99)

3. See p. 93, line 29.

4. See p. 93, last 2 lines and p. 94, line 1.

5. See p. 94, para. 2.

6. See p. 95, line 1.

7. See p. 96, para 4.

8. (a) See Acts 18.2.
(b) See Acts 18.3.
(c) See Acts 18.19
(d) See Acts 18.24–25.
(e) See Acts 18.27–28.

9. (a) See p. 32, last line and p. 33, lines 1–2.

10. (a) v. 8.
(b) See 1 Cor. 16.17.
(c) See 1 Cor. 16.10.
(d) See 1 Cor. 16.12.

11. The writer changes the subject suddenly, and in these verses deals with Christians being associated with immoral people. In 1 Cor. 5.9 Paul says, 'I wrote you in my letter not to associate with immoral men'.

Pages 105–106

2. See p. 100, para. 4.

3. See p. 100, para. 3.

4. See p. 102, para. 3.

5. See p. 103, para. 3.

6. See p. 103, Section on Ephesians.
(a) para. 2; (b) para. 1.

8. See Philemon 22.

11. See Col. 1,17; 4.12.

12. See Eph. 2.19–22; 4.15–16; 1 Cor. 3.9–11; 12.4–27.

136

Pages 111–112

3. See p. 106, last para.
4. See p. 107, Section on Hebrews, line 4.
5. See p. 108, para. 3.
6. See p. 108, Section on Two Letters to the Dispersion.
7. See p. 109, para. 1.
8. See p. 107, para. 1 and p. 111, paras. 2 and 3.
9. See 1 John 1.6,8,10; 2.4,6,9.
11. See Hebrews 13.
12. They were losing heart and growing weak.
14. See 1 Peter 5.
16. See p. 55, para. 3.

Chapter 8: Eschatology (Pages 116–117)

1. (a) See p. 113, chapter title.*
   (b) See p. 113, Section on Apocalyptic Writing, line 4.*
   (c) See p. 116, lines 1–3.*
3. See p. 113, last two paras. and p. 114, lines 1–6.
4. See p. 114, line 2.
5. See p. 113, lines 7–3 from foot of page.
6. See p. 116, para. 3.
7. Rev. 3.3 is in the future tense. Rev. 16.15 is in the present tense.
8. (a) It will be a day of resurrection for believers.
   (b) In Jesus resurrection is a reality now.
   (c) Jesus is Saviour, not judge, but people will be judged by the words He spoke.
9. 'That day'.
10. The Israelites expected to be rewarded by God and to triumph over their enemies. Amos said that it would be a day of punishment and darkness for them.
11. (a) See Dan. 8.3,20.
    (b) See Dan. 8.5–8, 21.
    (c) See Dan. 8.9–12, 23–25.

Pages 122–123

3. (a) See p. 119, para. 2, line 5.
   (b) See p. 119, para. 1, lines 4–8.

137

(c) See p. 118, para. 4, lines 10–11.
(d) See p. 119, para. 2, lines 2–3.
4. See p. 118, para. 3, lines 8–12.
6. See Acts 10.1–2; 13.7; 21.30–40; 23.16–26; 27.1–3.
7. See 1 Peter 2.13–17.
8. 3 = The divine number (The Holy Trinity).
4 = The created world.
7 = Completeness and perfection (3 plus 4).
6 = Incompleteness.
12 = Completeness and perfection (3 multiplied by 4).
9. Twelve thousand from each of the twelve tribes of Israel (the number twelve symbolizing its completeness).

Pages 126–127
2. See p. 116, paras. 2 and 3; p. 123, paras. 2 and 3.
3. (a) See p. 123, para. 2, line 2.
(b) See p. 125, para. 1, lines 2–5.
4. See p. 125, para. 3.
5. See p. 126, para. 2.
6. See 2 Peter 3.3–4.
7. (a) See Jer. 29.10.
(b) See Jer. 29.5–7.
8. They had lost their enthusiasm and sense of urgency.

Index

This index includes most of the subjects dealt with in this Guide, and the names of important people and places mentioned. Page numbers with an asterisk refer to the Glossary, where certain words are defined more fully than in the text.. Numbers in italic type refer to the maps.